CONCEIVING the INCONCEIVABLE

FULFILLING THE DREAM

David H. Johnston

Copyright © 2023 David H. Johnston
All rights reserved
First Edition

NEWMAN SPRINGS PUBLISHING
320 Broad Street
Red Bank, NJ 07701

First originally published by Newman Springs Publishing 2023

Cover design by Alex Jaeger

ISBN 978-1-68498-217-2 (Paperback)
ISBN 978-1-68498-218-9 (Digital)

Printed in the United States of America

To Marianna, my wife, and mother
of my children—Dietrich David,
Noel Hampton, and Melissa "Missy" Michelle

CONTENTS

Chapter 1: In the Beginning 1
Chapter 2: Of Mice and Men 5
Chapter 3: Looking for a Job 9
Chapter 4: Wedding Bells? 12
Chapter 5: Summers of Performing 16
Chapter 6: Two Worlds: Education / Music Ministry 18
Chapter 7: The Eye of the Needle 21
Chapter 8: The Road Ahead 24
Chapter 9: It's a Girl! 28
Chapter 10: Restless 30
Chapter 11: Conceiving the Inconceivable 32
Chapter 12: The Visit and Birth 38
Chapter 13: Feast of Tabernacles 45
Chapter 14: Off and Running 50
Chapter 15: Too Stubborn to Quit 57
Chapter 16: A Place of Beginning Again 68
Chapter 17: Extending the Borders 71
Chapter 18: And the Winner Is… 74
Chapter 19: International Educator of the Year 78
Appendix A 83
Appendix B 87
Appendix C 89
Appendix D 91

CHAPTER 1

In the Beginning

It was a dark time in US history when our president gave the order to enter World War II. Our commander in chief, President Franklin Delano Roosevelt, led the US military in defeating Adolf Hitler and the Nazi regime in Germany.

In the same year, the Nazis acknowledged their first failure on the war front at the Battle of Stalingrad. Regardless of this substantial German loss, World War II continued for two additional years.

In the same year, Hitler had ordered the execution of six million Jews and declared Berlin free of them. Two years later, in 1945, Roosevelt gave the order to drop the atomic bomb on Hiroshima and Nagasaki, which led to the surrender of Japan.

Against this backdrop, my parents, Noble and Dessie B, in their late teens, met, fell in love, and married in Pontotoc, Oklahoma, on December 20, 1928. The new Mr. and Mrs. Noble Haskell Johnston started their lives together in not the best of times economically. Before they were married, Dad worked tirelessly planting a cornfield only to come home one afternoon to discover his dad had sold his entire crop claiming the money was needed to support the family. It wasn't difficult for Dad's sisters, who had already moved to California, to convince my parents to move there as well. Mom and Dad loaded their Model T, which Dad referred to as his "machine," as well as every other car he ever owned, and headed west to California.

Ten Days later, they arrived in Southern California and at first, they stayed with my Dad's sister, Florida, then later with another sister, Flossie, both in Willowbrook. The following year, in 1930, my mother gave birth to my oldest sister, Wilma, in Compton, California.

Since Dad had become a skilled welder, he was able to secure employment in the shipyards almost immediately after their arrival. Things had been tough for them as they arrived just in time for the Great Depression.

Very few healthy young men in the country dodged the draft, but because my dad was a welder and worked in the shipyards, the government and draft board deemed him a greater asset as a welder in the shipyards than serving in the military.

Twins—Dessie B and Bessie A

My mother, Dessie B, had an identical twin sister, Bessie A. Growing up, they were inseparable. What happened to one happened to the other. When one got married, the other followed suit shortly thereafter. They each had four children relatively at the same time. They were so close in so many ways. Their physical similarities were almost uncanny, even the small mole each of them had above the upper lip on the left side. They wore their hair the same, dressed alike, and had the same glasses frames. They had a lot of fun trying to fool us kids by pretending to be the other. I clearly recall the time

CONCEIVING THE INCONCEIVABLE

Aunt Bessie was giving me instructions to do something as if she were my mother. I didn't even suspect she was my aunt and not my mom. She had me fooled!

I was born in Compton, California, in 1943 and was the fourth and last child born with three older siblings—Wilma; a brother, Zandell; and another sister, Ruby. Wilma and Zandell were basically grown and already out of the house and living independently when our mother delivered Ruby and me. I've heard it said it was like having two families.

I remember Ruby playing the steel guitar in early childhood. Later in elementary school, she took bass lessons. But the music teacher needed cellists, so she made the transition from bass to the cello. Ruby only knew how to live happily; so growing up, for me, holds nothing but fun and happy memories of my childhood. By the time I was in high school, we had moved to Whittier, where I attended Whittier High School but only for my sophomore year.

I recall going to kids' camp from church and feeling a sense of call to Christian ministry when I grew up. And having started taking violin lessons in fourth grade under the renowned string pedagogue Ralph Matesky, I would also go to music camp during the summers. I remember that I wanted to become a professional violinist when I grew up, so thinking I would go into both the ministry and the field of music, I just accepted the fact that I would have to live my life in two different worlds.

In order to train for the ministry, I thought it would be important to attend Bible college, but I was unable to find a college or university that also offered training for serious students in violin performance. Thinking beyond high school, I figured I would be enrolling in a music school and would possibly have a difficult time developing knowledge and skill in the ministry. So I somehow convinced my parents to allow me to attend a Christian boarding high school in Canyonville, Oregon, for my last two years of high school. This decision was made with the intent of shaping me into the person God wanted me to be and grounding me in my faith. There were slogans all around the campus, one of which I still apply to everything I do:

"Only one life, 'twill soon be past. Only what's done for Christ will last."

It was in the first year of boarding school, my junior year, during Easter vacation, that my mother unexpectedly passed away during an unsuccessful open-heart surgery. For years, I blamed myself for her death, thinking I had broken her heart for leaving home when I was only sixteen years old. It spurred me on to work hard and become all that would have made her proud of me. Although I didn't have a private violin tutor in Canyonville, I still practiced as hard as I could every day.

Following high school graduation, I remember waiting at the Canyonville bus stop with my violin and one suitcase not knowing if I should take a bus north to Eugene, where I had applied to attend the University of Oregon School of Music, or south to Los Angeles, where I had applied to Cal State Los Angeles to major in music education. It was uncertain where I would be able to live in either place. I had two options: to stay with the family of one of my high school classmates in Lebanon, Oregon, or with a friend of my sister's in LA until I could find a place of my own.

Since I had not heard the results of my audition and application at the University of Oregon, it was simply a process of elimination, and I headed for LA. It was unfortunate for me that my father remarried later in the same year of my mother's passing to a woman to whom he gave his word that there would be no family members living in the same house with them, so I was not allowed nor welcomed there. I had no choice but to find my own place to live.

Years later, I discovered why I never heard from the University of Oregon. I made this discovery when I was playing in an orchestra under the baton of the famed conductor Bruno Walter at the Shrine Auditorium in Los Angeles. My desk partner just happened to mention she was a graduate of the University of Oregon Conservatory. When I told her my story of auditioning and never hearing from them, she asked me what year that was. When I told her it was 1961, she enlightened me by explaining that my records would have been lost in the fire later that year. The conservatory burned to the ground, and all the documents were destroyed.

CHAPTER 2

Of Mice and Men

God had His hand on me as I look back. Somehow, doors just opened for me to meet the right people who had positive Christian values and opportunities to study with exceptionally fine music teachers, including some of the world's leading string pedagogues. Alice Schoenfeld at USC and Ralph Matesky at the University of the Pacific had profound influences on my life, as well as imparting violin performance skills.

Gospel Notes: Carrie Mones, Oogie Schmitt, David Johnston, Barbara Ohanesian, Donna Schmitt, Paula Scott, Verna Kuderian, Jack Herron, Bob Ohanesian. Los Angeles, California—1962

I had learned from my parents that you become like the person or people with whom you spend most of your time. That first summer after high school graduation, I met a group of students around my age who were into evangelism as a singing group, the Gospel Notes. Verna was an art major and had just graduated from USC. Her sister, Donna, started attending LA State University the same semester I did. Jack was engaged to Verna; and Deril, whom everyone referred to as Oogie, was engaged to Donna. Along with other members of the group, they became my family. I will always be indebted to them for modeling and imparting spiritual values and living exemplary Christian lives.

Losing my mother when I was sixteen totally altered the trajectory and my carefully made plans for my life. I had to support myself, pay rent, buy food, and pay for private violin lessons, not to mention the crippling grief I carried for years. I was attending classes at California State University, Los Angeles, but the violin teacher I wanted was on the faculty at USC. I was able to audition at USC and was awarded a full scholarship but still had to come up with $500 for registration, which was a lot of money back in the day. I actually asked my dad if he could pay that fee for me; but he had fallen under the spell of his new wife, who was of the opinion that, if I didn't pay for everything myself, including registration fees, I wouldn't appreciate my education.

I sensed my dad really wanted to help me, but the pressures from his wife were stronger than his desire to assist me financially. There was one thing he did for me. He gave me the family car, a 1955 blue-and-white Chevy. It was a lifesaver for me as I needed transportation for going to work and all the things and places a college student would be required to attend. In my freshman year, the car was in need of repair beyond what I could afford, so I traded it in on a '59 VW Bug, which was promptly named Flattery. Although Flattery, as the name implied, would get me nowhere, it was actually quite reliable.

Whenever I made an appeal to my dad for financial assistance, the answer was always the same: "You just need to go part-time and take longer to get your degree." Problem was that I had already been classified 1A with the draft board, and only full-time students had a hope of postponing the report date for the physical. Had I changed my student status to part-time, I would have most assuredly been drafted and sent to Vietnam. A good number of my friends were sent there and came back in body bags. I was hoping God had other plans for me. I figured, What good am I to God in a body bag?

I continued as a full-time student and somehow managed to delay being drafted into the military. I applied to the US government to leave the country to study at the Mozarteum in Salzburg after my junior year and was granted a deferment and subsequently was able to spend three months in Europe. I had sent an audition tape some months earlier to enter the prestigious music school in Salzburg, Austria. While attending the Mozarteum, I had the good fortune of participating in the master class of Jean Fournier and serving as concertmaster of the festival orchestra. Apparently it is rare for performing artists to perform the works of Mozart in Salzburg, the city associated with the famed historic figure in music history. As it was known as the home of the great musical genius Wolfgang Amadeus Mozart, music critics tended to be pronouncedly opinionated as to the "authentic" Mozartian style. Consequently one would rarely hear anyone performing the more familiar and standard repertoire of Mozart.

Select students from the Fournier master class were chosen to perform at the end of the course in the Wiener Sal (Hall of Vienna), a rather smallish classical concert hall within the Mozarteum. Little did I know I would be walking into a den of lions when I chose to perform the Mozart no. 5, A dur, Violin Concerto (first movement only). Just before walking on stage, I was told that the performance would be a *live* broadcast on Austrian national television and the crown princess of Holland was in the audience. I just took a deep breath and proceeded to make my entrance on the stage. I was doing fine until I noticed my teacher, Jean Fournier, sitting in the balcony staring down at me. I would be lying if I said that didn't make me very nervous.

All said and done, I loved my studies and being in Salzburg during that summer.

Working a full-time job at Rockview Dairy in Downey, California, and attending classes, practicing, and teaching a few private students on Saturdays, I managed after four years of hard work and being stretched and considered it nothing short of a miracle that I successfully completed a bachelor's degree. My private violin teacher, Ralph Matesky, firmly insisted that I at least audition for the graduate fellowship offered by the University of the Pacific and enter a master's degree and teaching credential program. Auditions were held at the Biltmore Hotel in Los Angeles. I thought it was miraculous that I had finished a BA degree while working full-time and wasn't that interested in continuing and working toward a graduate qualification, but God had other plans.

I was already carrying some student loans and other debts and couldn't bear the thought of incurring even more. The draft was also hanging over my head, yet I knew I should at least try and get a paying job somewhere and begin paying off my debts. Within a few days, a letter came informing me that I had been awarded the fellowship! That just wasn't in my plan. I soon realized what an honor it was to have been awarded the fellowship since only one was awarded each year.

I then packed my things, filled Flattery to the brim, and moved to Stockton in Central California to begin studies for the master's degree.

The University of the Pacific Conservatory master of music program was a two-year program, which I somehow managed to complete in one year, including a California K–12 life teaching credential. Upon completing the course, I still maintained my resolve not to enlist in the army. I had friends in the performing arts who enlisted, basing their decision to fulfill their active duty in the army orchestra but instead served as paratroopers.

CHAPTER 3

Looking for a Job

I was looking for a teaching job, but at that time, no school district was willing to risk hiring anyone who had not fulfilled their military obligations. If a teacher were drafted during an academic year, it would be too disruptive to the teaching program. At the last minute, the Sacramento City School District was desperately in need of an instrumental music teacher. It was offering a one-year, long-term substitute contract teaching instrumental music in various elementary schools. The title was "traveling instrumental music teacher." It was offered to me, and I took it! They knew about me through the Sacramento City School District music coordinator Norman Lamb. We became good friends from playing together in the Capitol Symphony in Sacramento. Norm was the principal violist, and I was a violinist in the orchestra. Before concerts, he would frequently borrow my fingernail clippers and my rosin in the green room.

Upon moving to Sacramento, I looked for a good church to attend. Some of my friends recommended that I try Bethel Temple. It was a larger church than I was used to, but I enjoyed playing in the orchestra during worship. Spiritually I was fed. A wife of one of the pastors introduced me to her sister, whom I found attractive. People would sometimes ask me if I had a girlfriend and considered marriage during my college years. I was so busy and goal oriented that I simply did not have time to think about anything of that nature. I had a list of the type of girls I would be looking for in the future.

Nonetheless, I had established three essential criteria and basic character traits I would require and be looking for in a life's partner:

intellectual, spiritual, and physical attraction. Some other attributes and values were desirable as well. After meeting this girl, I began to think God could be showing me His plan. Marianna Schmidt was her name. She came from a solid Christian heritage. Her parents were German Mennonites born in Ukraine who escaped during the revolution and worked their way across China to the United States. They arrived in San Francisco in 1929. Marianna was number six, born in Wasco, California, and is one of seven children; she was a Bible major in college. Marianna was not a professional musician like other girls I knew who would argue with me over the musical interpretation of a piece of music but had a depth of understanding and appreciation of the performing arts. Marianna was intelligent, beautiful, and an extraordinary cook and had a joyful disposition.

I finished teaching that academic year, 1966–1967, and miraculously had not heard from the draft board; so I accepted an offer to teach a second year in the same district, including junior high. In the meantime, my feelings toward this girl were growing stronger. We enjoyed being together. My roommate, Owen, and I would buy the groceries; and Marianna and her roommate, Mila Rae, would cook. We shared the same values and faith.

I fell in love with her. At this point, it was questionable if the feelings were mutual. I knew she loved ice cream, so I took her to an ice-cream parlor. As we sat across the table eating ice cream, I bypassed the traditional forms of marriage proposals and asked her if she would be the mother of my children. I'll never forget the sudden pale look of fear that fell upon her face.

Meanwhile, I could not see teaching elementary and junior high school as a long-term vocation. At the same time, I was still young and free; I would audition to enter a doctorate program at the Julliard School in New York. I'll not forget playing for a small panel that included the famed master Ivan Galamian and renowned teacher Dorothy Delay. I don't think I had ever been that nervous before, but I was motivated by my goal to teach at the college level. A doctorate was an essential requirement.

To enter the doctor of musical arts (DMA) program at Julliard required an invitation based on at least one year of enrollment as an undeclared graduate student. There would be no guarantee of being offered a place in the doctoral program, but I was still planning to commence my studies at Julliard.

CHAPTER 4

Wedding Bells?

While in New York, it became evident that absence does make the heart grow fonder. Upon returning to Sacramento to prepare for my move to New York, Marianna, the girl I was so attracted to, made overtures that made it clear that she could have feelings for me as I did for her.

At that time, I received a phone call from the president of Bakersfield College, Dr. Edward Simonsen. My mentor and teacher since I was nine years old, Ralph Matesky, gave Dr. Simonsen my name. Mr. Matesky was also primarily responsible for the award I received of the graduate fellowship at the University of the Pacific Conservatory. During my graduate studies, he was also my violin teacher and coached me in my preparation for my master's recital.

Bakersfield College Music Department had been searching for a string specialist and conductor for the college/community orchestra. The wheels began to turn at this point! After working on a doctorate at Julliard for four years and with the way the job market was going at that time and in the foreseeable future in the field of music in universities and colleges, I had doubts that I would be offered a better job than the professorship at Bakersfield College. So I accepted the invitation to join the faculty as an assistant professor of music at Bakersfield College. Thanks go to Ralph Matesky for his confidence and belief in me by recommending me for this position. Attending the Julliard School was put on the back burner. I wrote to Mr. Galamian and thanked him for listening to me play, for his valuable time, and for his advice. I will never forget it.

CONCEIVING THE INCONCEIVABLE

How could I just up and move to Bakersfield and leave my heart in Sacramento? So I asked Marianna to marry me and begin our lives together in Bakersfield at the start of the academic year. She said yes and expressed she wanted a big church wedding and thought we should wait a year to give her time to save money and plan. It took a week to convince her we should do it right away even though we had only three weeks left to make it happen within the necessary timeline. I summoned my sources, mainly my sister Ruby, and had the invitations printed and sent out in two days and dresses designed and made by my other sister, Wilma, and my niece Gwen. Other details were taken care of, including making reservations and flights to Oahu and Kauai for a ten-day honeymoon. We had a magnificent wedding ceremony on August 23, 1968, that fulfilled our hopes and dreams and beyond for both of us.

Wedding Day—August 23, 1968

Returning from our honeymoon, the inevitable and dreaded letter from the draft board appeared. At this point in my life, I had learned that, when there was a fork in the road and a decision had to be made as to which way to go, I would begin walking through an open door. If it were the wrong one, it would close, and God would have another path for me.

Moving from Sacramento to Bakersfield, I found myself physically on the dividing line between the Central and Southern jurisdictions for reporting for the US Army physical exam. The letter I received instructed me to report to the Central California location, and I replied and requested a change to the Southern jurisdiction. Since I now lived in the midway boundary, it was my right to request the change. I was expecting to hear from the military within a few days with instructions as to when and where to report for the physical examination in Southern California, but I never heard from them.

I'll never forget the joy I felt when Marianna announced she was pregnant. It was the year 1971 and the era when the baby's father was not allowed in the delivery room. Our baby was due on April 27, but he wasn't ready yet. So on the night of my dress rehearsal of the spring concert of the college community orchestra, April 29, our firstborn son came forth. We desired to have children with strong character, so we named him Dietrich. He has truly lived up to his name.

The following year at Christmastime, our second child was due on December 22. Since the birth of Dietrich, our first child, the hospital rules had changed; and if we took the Lamaze class, I would be allowed in the delivery room. I directed our church Christmas production, which had its last performance on Christmas Eve. We had a few people over after the production; and when the last couple left, I recall being exhausted, lying on the floor and telling Marianna I was finally free for her to have the baby anytime. She didn't answer. I looked up and saw she was doing one of the Lamaze exercises and couldn't speak. I asked her if she was just practicing, and she shook her head in a silent no in response. We got in the car and headed for the hospital!

It was late December 24, 1972. Since we were a Lamaze couple, the hospital staff pretty much left us alone to do our breathing exercises and the coaching techniques I had practiced. At one point, a nurse tossed a pair of green pants and a top on a chair in our labor room. She apologized for only having extra-large-sized pants.

She said, "Here, put these on."

No one had given me instructions about this; so I did what I was told, took off my clothes, and put on the extra-large green garments. Even though the green pants had a drawstring, they were still huge and uncomfortable. I actually had difficulty keeping them up.

Marianna's heavy labor lasted for more than ten hours. When I could see the baby's head crowning, I knew it was time to go to the delivery room! We had learned from our Lamaze class that, if a baby was born outside a sterile area, you would be charged for a private room. I was yelling for help, but no one came. I thought, if I had to deliver this baby, I would wheel my wife into the delivery room myself! I then quickly pulled up the side rails on her gurney and burst into the hallway on our way down the hall to the delivery room. I made it as far as the nurses' station when my extra-large green pants fell below my knees. I didn't care; I just kept going with Marianna on the gurney as fast as I could go while listening to the giggling nurses. It would have helped if the nurse had instructed me to put the green pants over the top of my clothes!

I got the attention needed as I quickly rolled her into the delivery room. Dr. Anderson walked into the room still wearing his sport coat, which he wore when he delivered the baby. Early Christmas morning, our son, Noel, was born.

Almost two years passed when our senior pastor, Harold Bither, announced he had accepted the position of senior pastor at the Assembly of God church in Pomona in Southern California. I was invited to go with the ministry team in Bakersfield and serve as the music minister at Pomona First Assembly.

I enjoyed my time at the college lecturing in music history, conducting the college community orchestra, and taking classes in German and French to prepare for my qualifying exams should I have the opportunity to pursue a doctorate down the road.

CHAPTER 5

Summers of Performing

Marianna and I both were fortunate to have jobs that gave us the flexibility of expanding our horizons during the summer months. Our first summer together, we spent ten weeks traveling in Europe, including a few weeks of chamber music and conducting at the Mozarteum in Salzburg, Austria.

A good friend from the Sacramento City School District and principal viola of the Capitol Symphony, Norman Lamb, knew the music contractors for the local musicians' union in the Reno / Lake Tahoe districts. He made repeated suggestions that I make myself known to them so I possibly would be invited to play in an orchestra for one of the shows for a famous entertainer. He said it would be a good experience and I could earn a little extra money.

After our firstborn, Dietrich, it was summertime in 1972. We drove to Sparks, Nevada, to visit Marianna's sister, Riki, the wife of Frank Mapes, a former associate pastor at Bethel Temple, the church I attended in Sacramento. Sparks is near Reno. We stayed with them until we could rent a place of our own on the South Shore of Lake Tahoe. There was a risk of not being hired to play a gig until all local union musicians were contracted. To be a local member of the musicians' union, I would have to be a transfer member for three months, and I was only able to be there for one. We still thought it was worth a shot as Marianna was expecting our second child and we needed the money. I thought, if nothing else, it would be a good experience and an exciting adventure.

I had just finished calling and speaking with all the music contractors in all the clubs in Lake Tahoe and Reno, letting them know of my availability and experience. The phone rang, and it was John Acton, the first contractor I called and the first on my list to contact. He asked if I could sight-read, and without any sense of boasting, I said yes. He went on to explain that the *Bobbi Gentry* show was opening that night at Harrah's Reno. Unfortunately, the violinist in the orchestra had just suffered a burst appendix and was rushed to Reno's hospital emergency for an appendectomy. Among the local union players, there wasn't one amongst them John was willing to hire due to their lack of expertise and ability to sight-read the charts. He thought it would be better to gamble on me rather than use one of the local union players.

I played the show that night with no rehearsal, which proved to be an easy task for me. The show ran for one week, and apparently having made a good impression on the music director and because the next show opening at Harrah's required an additional violin in the score, I was invited to stay on to play forty-two shows for the *Jerry Lewis Show* at Harrah's Reno! Words cannot express how much fun that was for me!

I ended up playing for lots of famous entertainers over the ensuing weeks that summer—two shows each night. I had the privilege of playing for Perry Como, Sammy Davis Jr., Steve Lawrence and Eydie Gorme, Bobby Vinton, Foster Brooks, Don Rickles, Liz Torres, Bobbi Gentry, Ann-Margaret, and the Carpenters. I especially enjoyed meeting and getting to know some of these remarkably talented and famous people.

There were other summers when I had the privilege of studying and performing at the Aspen Arts Festival and summer of chamber music in Idyllwild. In Idyllwild, we stayed in a small camper trailer with our boys, when they were very small, and I would practice in a cramped space with my bow hitting the ceiling of the camper. Marianna was a real trooper coping with the children and with all that was going on in such a cramped space.

The enjoyment of learning under some of the greatest masters and playing with other talented musicians made it all worth it!

CHAPTER 6

Two Worlds: Education / Music Ministry

Now that I had experience teaching at the elementary school level, junior high, high school, then the community college level, I realized my preferred age group was working with collegiate-level students. So after five years as an associate professor at Bakersfield College, I realized I had greater fulfillment teaching at the college/university level. A major hurdle in achieving that goal was the fact that I did not have a doctorate.

We were settled in Bakersfield. Marianna was teaching sixth grade; and in addition to teaching at the college, I had become the choir director in our church, which I also enjoyed. At that time, the pastor of our church announced he had accepted the position in Southern California at the First Assembly of God church in Pomona as senior pastor. I was invited to go with the Bakersfield ministry team and serve as the music minister at the church in Pomona. I've never been sorry I accepted that invitation.

Although I enjoyed my time at Bakersfield College lecturing and conducting, it was the end of my leave of absence, and I had to decide. At the time of my leave application to the academic board at Bakersfield College, we all thought it was only for one year. There were more than thirty applicants for my position, all PhD candidates, knowing it was only for my one-year leave of absence. I thought, if I didn't return and continue with my tenured position at the college, it would be closing a door behind me; and I would surely never be able to resume such a position again.

Finding myself at another fork in the road, I applied my guiding motto once again: "Only one life, 'twill soon be past. Only what's done for Christ will last." It really helped to clarify my decision. Although more financially secure, I somehow felt that returning to Bakersfield would be a dead end for me, which I would be trading for the stimulus and fulfillment I was enjoying in Southern California. The college president, Dr. Edward Simonsen, realized what was at stake concerning my future and made me an offer to take a second-year leave of absence.

While I deeply appreciated Dr. Simonsen's generous offer, I resigned from my position at Bakersfield College and continued with my studies at the University of Southern California.

When I was in elementary school, my parents would send me to kids' camp, a summer program of the church. After I began to demonstrate that I was taking music seriously through violin practice, my parents would also send me to music camp. After church camp, I made a promise to God that I would work for Him all my life.

Likewise, after music camp, I thought, *That's it! I'm going to play violin professionally and perform as my career.*

I was committed to both and thought to keep my vow to God and to myself; I just had to live my life in two different worlds.

It appeared I was destined to live my life in what I thought were two worlds, Christian ministry and the world of education and as a professional musician. I considered myself fortunate not to have parents that tried to push me into a profession they wanted me to pursue but allowed me to decide for myself. My mother always told me, whatever field I chose, to just make sure it was something that helped others. Together with God's call on my life, I can't imagine living without music and playing the violin. Teaching music has helped young people to have a life of greater fulfillment, including the expansion of mental capabilities, enabling them to excel academically.

Pursuing both ministry and the arts satisfied every requirement, including my resolve to live out my high school motto: "Only one life, 'twill soon be past. Only what's done for Christ will last." Some years later, I realized that God made me just the way I am, and He intended for me to live in only one world and incorporate all aspects of my life. Education leads to freedom. We were designed to be free. God is the giver of talent and every perfect gift. When we hear a brilliant performing artist, it is sometimes said, "That performer is gifted." During the time I was at Julliard, I spoke with a talented and brilliant undergraduate violin major and asked him why he was so motivated to become a renowned, world-class violinist.

His reply was "I have to become great. Otherwise, it will break my grandfather's heart, and I can't possibly let him down!"

When knowledge leads to understanding that we were created for the pleasure of God, our motivation is purposed to please the heart of our Heavenly Father. Nothing could be a higher calling! Thus, the conception of a college that integrated the arts and Christian precepts and knowledge of God's Word. It's a college I would have chosen to attend, but it didn't exist anywhere in the world at the time.

CHAPTER 7

The Eye of the Needle

In 1968, when Marianna and I were first married and had moved to Bakersfield and started our new jobs, we both agreed that it was very important to commit to a local church. Both of us had come from an Assembly of God background, so we quickly discovered that Bakersfield First Assembly at Seventeenth and O was the place to go. We immediately felt at home there and made lifelong friendships. I had always been critical of choirs and didn't care much for choral music because I couldn't stand the sound of untrained voices and mediocrity in music performance whether choral or instrumental! For some reason, almost every choir I heard had pitch problems, and the sound was just not pleasing to my ears. I clearly recall being stunned by the excellence of the church choir at Bakersfield First Assembly. It wasn't a particularly large group of singers. They weren't formally trained, but they were gifted singers. It was a pleasure to listen to a group with such natural talent.

    We hadn't been attending the church very long when the music pastor, Don Stover, announced that he had accepted a position with Lexicon Music Publishers working with Ralph Carmichael. Harold Bither and the other members of the pastoral team had already moved to Southern California and started their new ministry in Pomona. Fred Cottrell, our new pastor at Bakersfield First Assembly, approached me to ask if I would fill in as the interim music director for the church until the board could conduct a search for a new one to replace the previous one. I thought about it and decided I would like to have the experience of working with such gifted voices. Besides, I thought it would only be for a couple of months.

More than a year had passed, and it was clear that the church was not interested in finding a new music minister. The fact remained that I liked working with the music in the Bakersfield church, and the church liked me and had no plans to find a replacement. Regardless of the satisfaction and enjoyment of teaching and working with my college orchestra and the music in the church, we decided to purchase a house and move to Upland. It was announced that I would be the new music minister and worship leader at Pomona First Assembly.

It was during the academic year of 1976 that I was fortunate enough to attend a worship symposium in Dallas, Texas. Since I had become the worship pastor at our church during the time it met at Upland High School Auditorium, I wanted to learn as much as I could about worship leading. There were workshops and guest speakers from other countries, including David and Dale Garratt from Australia and Mike and Viv Hibbert from New Zealand. On the final evening of the symposium, there was a formal dinner held in the ballroom of the Dallas Cowboy Stadium. During the course of worship that evening, there was a prophetic message that came forth from a local pastor, Charlotte Baker. She spoke with clarity and verbal skill that made every word penetrate the minds and into the hearts of those who heard her speak.

The evening was the grand finale of the symposium week, and by that point during the symposium, I was open to receiving anything that God would have for me. Never before or since have I heard anything like it. Pastor Baker began by describing a person who was just like me, ready to be a vessel of the Holy Spirit, to enter into deep and genuine worship. Throughout the prophetic word, Kirk Dearman was prophesying on the piano, mirroring the spoken words of Pastor Baker.

I had been playing my violin in the orchestra during worship that evening and was sitting there holding my instrument when she began to speak. She began by describing someone standing at the gate of worship who asked God for an education that led to advanced degrees and God granting the desires of his or her heart. Then she described that the same person was still not satisfied and asked God for a beautiful instrument and to impart the ability to perform sweetly in worship to God. So God again granted the desires of his or her heart. By now, it was too obvious to me that she couldn't be talking about anyone else there that night other than me.

I thought, *How could God single out one person in the midst of such a large crowd of people like that?*

I could not deny that it was happening. It was unmistakable. She went on to say that, although God continued to grant the desires of my heart, I still desired more.

Then I expressed, as I was standing at the gate of worship, that my desire was to enter through the gate, but I couldn't make it through as it was a very small and narrow gate. Then I heard God say, in order for me to enter the gate, I had to lay down my books of learning and my instrument and bow down low in order to make it through. I then laid down my 1715 Testore violin on the floor and fell down with my face on the ground. It was only then I understood that God only wanted me to be in His presence without holding on to any of the things that had been granted to me. I really can't say how long I was there in that position, but I know I was unable to speak for a couple of hours.

Later that night, when riding in the car on the way to the home where I was staying during the symposium, I heard someone say that it was awesome to witness more than a hundred people on their faces in God's presence. I was stunned when I heard that because I actually thought I was the only one.

CHAPTER 8

The Road Ahead

Relocating to Southern California enabled me to enroll at USC to begin work on my doctorate in violin performance and music education. It was 1977; and I was working at the church, studying at USC, and practicing. Alice Schoenfeld was an inspiring violin teacher. What more could I possibly ask for? My studies at USC were so enriching and relevant to what I was doing and what I hoped to be doing in the future. I loved my studies at the university!

In one of my classes, we were expected to incorporate our studies with our place of employment, which, for me, was the church. Part of that unit was to confront the weakness of most performing artists who generally lacked verbal communication skills. They would rather stand in front of an audience of thousands and perform a concerto with an orchestra rather than speak at a board meeting and convince the board to spend the money to purchase better equipment for their music department at a school, church, or where they were teaching.

In my case, our church desperately needed an adequate sound system. One of our deacons built the existing system some years prior to my arrival. It consisted of a couple of speakers placed on the platform facing the congregation of 1,500 with one dial controlling the volume, which was mounted on the arm of a pew. It was, however, on an aisle seat where he sat to control the volume with a singular small dial. I never knew of a service or a performance with our eighty-voice choir and orchestra when the system didn't frequently destroy the atmosphere that had just been so beautifully created by the orchestra and choir with ear-piercing feedback.

I prepared my presentation with a solid rationale and successfully convinced the board to invest a sizable sum of money into upgrading the sound system. The deacon who built the existing system was not happy! The last debate was over how the new speakers would be enclosed. We fortunately were able to compromise by hanging the cluster of speakers in a custom-made central enclosure. It, however, did resemble a white casket! To this day, it is referred to as David's Tomb. At least I got an A on that assignment!

In the same class at USC where the students were encouraged to integrate the subjects into their place of employment, it wasn't too difficult for me at my church since I had already developed thirteen graded choirs; taught private and group lessons on Saturdays, which we called the Saturday Conservatory of Pomona (SCOP), and handbell choirs to teach music reading; and launched a Suzuki program in our preschool. I directed a high school music and drama group, which we called the Red Letter Edition. The students in this group took their ministry seriously and were trained for evangelism as well as singing, movement, and acting. I took this performing arts group on tour around the country every other year, and in the alternate years, we would tour internationally.

Red Letter Edition. The photo was taken at the Los Angeles County Arboretum in Arcadia, California 1977

The Red Letter Edition, made up of around forty-five young people, toured the country of Australia performing and ministering in churches and universities in 1980 with a follow-up tour in 1982. The second tour was made up of almost exclusively a production created by Colin Harbinson, a former YWAM director from Cambridge, Canada, called *Toymaker and Son*. He originally wrote and choreographed the production with a blend of drama, mime, music, and dance for his students in middle school. A few months later, the first public performance was premiered with an adult cast in the Piazza San Marco in Venice, Italy. It went on to be performed in over seventy countries.

Toymaker and Son is an allegory of the Gospel. The toymaker represents the father, and the son is cast as a younger male actor who relates to the toymaker as if he were his father. The father tries to protect his son; but the teddy bears, called the Cruel Teds, lie and try to trick the son and the other toys. They also beat up the son when he doesn't do what they want, attempting to instill fear in the eyes and hearts of all the inhabitants of Toyland. The Cruel Teds, who are inspired by the apprentice (the evil one), convince all the toys in Toyland to rebel against the toymaker and destroy the son by nailing him against a wall made of blocks until he dies. The sun rises, and on the third day, the son comes alive again drawing all the toys who want to be with him to his side. He was the only one who could repair the toys and restore Toyland, but sadly some of the toys had chosen to be loyal to the apprentice who told them it was a lie. There was a battle, and the son conquers the apprentice. The son then repairs and restores the toys that were broken and hurt, bringing peace and joy once again to Toyland.

CONCEIVING THE INCONCEIVABLE

Toymaker and Son cast—Red Letter Edition—Australian Tour 1982. Lisa Ferris, Leanne Danley, Paul Van Houwelingen, Brian Madsen, Willie Schmidt, Margaret Barber, John Melendez, Dale Gayman, Ron Smith, Leighton Sheley

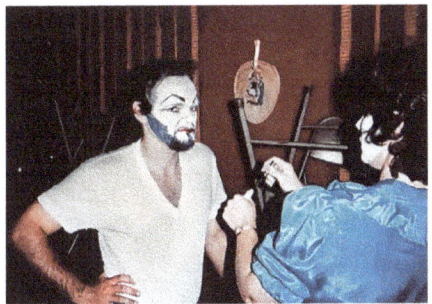

David playing the role of the Apprentice in Toymaker and Son—Christine Fillipowicz, nee Terrien choreographer, and makeup Designer from Cambridge, Canada YWAM

Toymaker and Son live performance at the University of Queensland

CHAPTER 9

It's a Girl!

In the meantime, my beautiful wife had given birth to two boys in Bakersfield. She was now a stay-at-home wife and mother—a big job.

In 1978, God blessed us with a third child, Melissa. I asked God for a healthy baby above all, but it would be so special to have a little girl we could call Missy. Again God granted the desires of my heart, and Missy was born on July 20, 1978.

It was a busy time of the year, with the church music department preparing for the annual Easter production.

Missy was twenty months old when, one day, I was working in my office and received a call from the doctor at the Kaiser Clinic, where Marianna had taken Missy that morning. She was listless and had a high fever. It was a call from the doctor who strongly suggested I make my way to the hospital immediately. She informed me that Missy was taken by ambulance to the Kaiser Hospital in Fontana. I instantly jumped in the car and made my way to the hospital, not knowing what I was going to hear when I got there.

The doctor met me and invited me into her office. She explained that our baby was in a coma and that I needed to prepare myself for possibly some bad news.

She said, "Your baby could die, and if she lives, she could have a wide range of disabilities, blindness, deafness, paralysis, and much more."

She had spinal meningitis and had to have intravenous feeding of three different drugs administered one at a time. She explained that, if she didn't get the right kind of drug, she could die and, if she got the wrong drug, it would kill her. Only by prayer and following her gut did the doctor know which drug to administer first.

Alice Moland, a member of my choir, came to the hospital to have a word with me. She said to carefully examine my heart and, if there was any way I had put my love and devotion of my little girl before God, I was to repent and give Missy up and let God heal her. I had an encounter with what Abraham must have felt when he was about to sacrifice Isaac. I had to give Missy back to God and let go. It was the hardest thing I'd ever had to do. There were five doctors working on Missy's case, and they all attributed Missy's fast and complete healing and recovery to the prayers of the members of the church. None of the side effects of her illness ever surfaced. A treasured keepsake given to us by Diana Norris, a valued member of my choir, is a commemorative plate called the Melissa plate, created and signed by the artist Frances Taylor Williams and cast and numbered in the year 1978, the year Missy was born. Inscribed on the back reads "Because of Jesus, I live."

CHAPTER 10

Restless

We loved our church. The people loved us. We were well taken care of. I had endless opportunities to express my creativity through productions, touring performing arts groups, and basically anything I wanted to do; but somehow, deep down, I knew there was something more God was calling me to do. I had become restless in my spirit and was becoming more and more unsettled. I felt like the baby eagle when its mother felt it was time to leave the nest and fly on its own. The mother's method was to make the nest so uncomfortable the baby eagle had no choice but to leave the nest and try its wings for the first time. Was that what was happening to me?

For so many years, I resisted making a commitment to working in a church as a full-time job because I saw the effects on the family, especially on the children. I could not go along with the notion of establishing one's children in a school and potentially making lifelong friends just to move away and take them out and disrupt their lives. I once heard a music minister say that, if things got uncomfortable for them in their church, they could always pull up stakes and find greener pastures. I could not go along with that philosophy.

Working in the church and being stimulated by classes at USC were so fulfilling for me I couldn't imagine ever leaving. Many of the students in Red Letter Edition frequently expressed their desire to leave their jobs and minister full-time through the group. It was at that time that a vision for full-time study of the Word of God combined with serious study of the performing arts had begun to grow within me. I realized there was no way I could start a Christian college of the arts, but the idea began to consume me.

Our church had a good facility and could have easily been adapted to serve as a college. There was adjoining vacant land on which a complex for the performing arts could be built.

As a project in one of my classes at USC, I prepared a presentation to the church to give birth to a Christian college of the arts funded by and under the banner of the church. The vision was presented to the board, and it was well received. It was noted, spoken by one of the board members, that "these things just don't happen overnight, and one has to be patient." Years went by, and it seemed my vision was going in the opposite direction. Repeatedly I was reminded of my high school slogan: "Only one life, 'twill soon be past. Only what's done for Christ will last."

I became restless and had thoughts thinking my life wasn't going to be ultimately fulfilled. That year, our annual Christmas banquet, sponsored by the church choir, was held at Griswold's in Claremont. An invitation was extended to Jack Hayford, pastor of Church on the Way in Van Nuys, to be our guest speaker. To go with the Christmas theme, Pastor Jack spoke on the concept of a book he was writing at the time entitled *The Mary Miracle*. As he was speaking, something was beginning to stir within me.

CHAPTER 11

Conceiving the Inconceivable

> *As with a pregnancy, everything in life starts with a possibility and proceeds to a reality. The pattern of conception-to-delivery is rooted in the founding fundamentals of God's operational order of things. And life is always a miracle.*
> —Jack Hayford,
> *The Mary Miracle*
> (Regal Book, 1994)

The night of the Christmas banquet was upon us, and Pastor Jack Hayford spoke.

He started out by saying something like, "I'm inviting you to travel with me to a dry, drab, and barren uninviting town of Nazareth and to review how God is able to bring life into the most barren settings and to breathe hope into the most unpromising situations.

"Try to picture the setting of the time when Mary discovered she had been chosen to carry and give birth to the Savior of the world. Actually God doesn't need a setting. Was Mary at prayer or washing dishes? Was there a shaft of light upon her countenance or a streak of perspiration? Was she at a quiet, convenient time in her day, or was this encounter an interruption? Was she poised as though having a read of a script in advance or just plain frightened by the angel's sudden appearance?

"Had Mary's parents taught her she could be the one? Or had the thought never occurred to her? Was she the town beauty and socially adept or a plain girl with a simple faith?

"The story doesn't require an impressive résumé.

"She sang several days later, 'For He has regarded the lowly state of His maidservant. He has exalted the lowly. He has filled the hungry' (Luke 1:48, 52, 53)."

Somehow, I found myself projecting into each aspect of the story.

He went on to say, "This is not a Grimm's fairy-tale princess waiting to be discovered by her prince charming.

"Biblically she was like you and like me and was not born out of an immaculate conception. To be the mother of God, you would have to be highly regarded and chosen by God.

"She was uncluttered, unembellished, plain, and simple. The same way all of God's salvation processes work, without human invention and beyond human understanding. Mary's humanness is essential to fully appreciating her miracle."

It was not difficult to find a parallel analogy of myself within the context of the story. The story of Mary being God's chosen one was making my heart race and was beginning to impact me in ways that almost frightened me. It was like going to the rim of darkness and taking that one step beyond without knowing what I would discover.

The story continued, and he began explaining the unfathomable trust God would have had in Mary to carry His Son. In essence, when we receive the seed God plants within us, we are also carrying a representation and piece of Jesus. Mary could have aborted or decided not to go through with it. The risk of Mary being stoned or put to death was very real in that culture during that time. When she accepted the conception of the inconceivable, there were no immediate physical signs to show that it really happened. And so the process, including testing, began. What strength of character, commitment, and courage Mary had. Although there were no immediate signs of anything happening, the stretching and growing, dealing with rumors, and so many other challenges began.

Pastor Hayford, when wrapping up, asked if anyone felt they had received the seed of a call to ministry or a dream or a vision but thought it could be just a fantasy or a passing thought. I immediately thought of my dream of a full-time school where students could find their pursuit of excellence on their instrument integrated with the study of Scripture and building of their faith. I thought it was perfectly safe since no one knew what I was thinking. At that point, Pastor Jack invited everyone to stand and then asked if anyone felt they had a call from God to a ministry that would clearly fall in the category of beyond the realm of natural possibility. Then he asked for those people to hold their hands cupped in front of them and, by faith, receive the seed from the Holy Spirit conceiving the inconceivable.

Pastor Jack went on to explain that, if we were capable and able to fulfill that dream ourselves, it did not qualify. It had to be something that would unquestionably be considered a miracle for it to come to pass. We were also reminded that it was important with whom we shared our experience. Mary told no one at first, but as time passed, she had signs of affirmation. She went to Ein Karem to see her cousin, Elizabeth, in whom she could confide and who was also with child. When Mary walked into the room to see Elizabeth, who was pregnant with John the Baptist, Elizabeth felt her baby leap within her womb upon being in the presence of the Messiah within Mary's womb.

I can't say that I know anyone whose baby leaped in their womb when I walked into the room, but some amazing things did happen after the banquet that were difficult to explain. There were clear indications of God's affirmation that I had become pregnant with a vision for a Christian arts college.

I had been discussing it with the pastors and board over the years that we needed to build a college on our vacant land adjacent to the church property. But after years of sharing that vision and expressing my desire for it to come to pass, it was hard for me to think of the miracle seed I was carrying to be anything or anywhere beyond the status quo right there in Pomona.

After I spent years of training the Red Letter Edition, our high school / college performing arts team, and taking them on tour, an invitation came through the well-known missionary and evangelist to Brazil, Bernard Johnson, to minister in Australia. About a year into the planning of such a large undertaking to perform and minister throughout Australia, there was a change in the management of his organization. I received a letter from him explaining that it shouldn't have a bearing on our plans to come to Australia and, if we still felt led to go, he would introduce me to a pastor who was willing to do our itinerary, a pastor of a church in Townsville, David Cartledge.

I wrote to Pastor Cartledge to let him know we were still interested in coming. His response was encouraging and positive, so we made the decision to move forward with our plans to take the group to Australia. Along with a lot of prayer, fundraising, and use of savings, we managed to prepare and tour Australia in 1980. There were more than forty students who managed to raise the money in order to make the trip. The Red Letter Edition ministered in churches and universities in almost every state in Australia. The tour was successful and served to increase the passion and desire of many in the group that full-time study and ministry were what they desired.

Our first place of ministry on our itinerary was a fairly new church plant in Sydney, Christian Life Centre. Somehow the pastors became aware of what I was trying to do in Pomona, California. I found it interesting that this church also had the vision to start a Christian school of the arts. The pastor called me and expressed their desire to start such a school and asked if I wanted to be involved in some way. That wasn't exactly the question I was expecting; so I just asked for a copy of their course unit outlines, any curriculum they might have, administrative structure, means of funding, or anything else they had that I could read and make comments, thinking I might serve as an advisor.

About a week later, the same pastor called me again and said they actually had nothing in writing and offered to pay my way to Sydney to talk about it. My mind immediately thought they must have thought I would relocate there. I certainly was not remotely interested in moving with my family to the other side of the planet, so on the spot and as I did not want to be rude, all I could think of to say was that I would think about it.

My thoughts continued to be all consumed with the inception of a school of the arts built next to our property in Pomona and how we would find funding and what kind of a miracle story I would have to tell. Our church offices at this time were in Claremont, across the street from the travel agency that took care of all the travel arrangements for the Red Letter Edition over the previous decade. Since we were planning our next tour, I found cause to walk across the street to take care of some arrangements with Larry, our travel agent.

I said something to Larry that was totally out of character for me—something outrageous and bold.

I looked down at him sitting at his desk and said, "Larry, we have given your agency a lot of business over the years. I want you to give me a free round-trip ticket to Sydney, Australia."

He had a good laugh. I laughed, and everyone in his office laughed. I walked back to my office across the street, sat at my desk, and resumed work.

That afternoon, Larry walked across the street and into my office, which was highly unusual since he'd never been there before. He looked at me sitting at my desk and nonchalantly placed an envelope in front of me. He then went on to explain that, after I had left his office, he got a notification from Continental Airlines announcing they were starting a new service to Sydney and, as a promotion, his agency was offered two complimentary government escort passes on a return flight from Los Angeles to Sydney. As it turned out, they could only make use of one of them and wondered what they could do with the other. Since no one in the office could use it, he remembered that I had asked for a free ticket to Sydney.

"Well, here it is. Enjoy your trip!" he said.

Now I was beginning to get nervous. Was it a confirmation of something that happened at the banquet, or was it my imagination?

For as long as I could recall, I had always resisted going into full-time ministry after observing so many families become dysfunctional as a result of the transient nature of music ministry. There just was no stability for the kids moving around so much. So what was I thinking in entertaining the thought of moving to the other side of the world? I was asked to make a two-year commitment and figured, if it were just for two years, it would at least be an exciting adventure. Little did I know it would turn into twenty-eight years!

I had been concerned with getting back to the pastor of the church in Sydney that had insisted I fly down there at their expense. There was no way I was going to do that. I would have a sense of obligation to them had I accepted their generous offer. So rather than giving a blunt reply of rejection, I had put my impending reply to him on the back burner. With a free ticket, I felt totally free to make the trip and pay the pastor and his team the respect of at least discussing what vision they had for such a school without any sense of obligation. I breathed a big sigh of relief after making the call informing him of my arrival.

CHAPTER 12

The Visit and Birth

My arrival in Sydney was like a royal visit. Some of the pastors from the church were there to greet me at the airport and take me to my hotel. The arrival details were well organized and made me feel important. During the week, the senior pastor called a meeting every day with his executive staff and me to discuss, dream, and discover where the Holy Spirit might lead the conversation. My struggles for many years had been in heavy discussions with church board members who resisted even discussing the concept of starting a Christian college of the arts or even supporting the arts in the church. Here I felt the freedom to speak and dream. It was affirming to hear them ask the same questions I had before I realized I even had them. I was stunned by how like-minded and unified we were. I really don't know why these men of God thought I would be the one to start the school of the arts they were dreaming of or why they thought I was qualified. But for some strange reason, I kept going with the exchange and pondered it all in my heart.

After the second day, I actually began to think it may be possible for me to relocate there with Marianna and the kids for a short period of time at least until the college was underway. Could it be that in order to fulfill that which the Holy Spirit had planted in me that night of the banquet included uprooting my family from our beautiful home, kids from their school, and the security of being loved and well taken care of by a wonderful church family and move to the other side of the planet?

By the end of the week, I felt a clear calling from God to say yes to moving to Australia and to the invitation of starting the college based in Sydney at Christian Life Centre. I did feel it was necessary to explain to the pastors that the calling I felt was not enough for me to come and that they needed to pray that Marianna would receive an independent call from God to move there as well. She had always stayed by my side and supported me no matter what. I knew she would agree to go if I felt it was the thing to do, but I was not willing to take the responsibility of taking her away from her mom and dad and siblings and moving as far away as Australia.

When I returned home to Upland, I clearly recall walking up to our front door and knocking. Marianna opened the door; we embraced.

Then she said, "You don't have to tell me. God spoke to me in church on Sunday, and I know we are to go."

I was overcome with emotion as we both burst into tears and embraced in the entryway of our Upland home.

Words aren't enough to express the magnitude of the hundreds of details that followed to prepare for such a major move. There was the matter of who was going to take care of our house and dog, filing applications for each of us to gain permanent resident status in a foreign country, what to ship, and what to put in storage. The list was overwhelming.

David and Marianna with their kids before leaving for
Australia at our home in Upland—December 1982

Family arrival in Sydney, January 5 1983

One year later, on January 7, 1983, upon our arrival in Sydney, we were taken to the Riverview Apartments in Lane Cove, where we stayed for two months while looking for an appropriate house to rent in the best area for the kids to attend public school.

Our oldest, Dietrich, was eleven at this time. He was taken out of Citrus Elementary School halfway through grade 6.

I often said to our friends, "You could still see the skid marks in the Pacific Ocean by dragging him to Australia."

It was the first time attending a school where there was a mandate to wear school uniforms; and because of his age, he was put directly into grade 7, which, in Sydney, was high school. He also had to take public transport, which none of our kids had done before. On the first day when coming home after school on the bus, someone was told to inform our son when to get off to get to our house. He should have been home by three thirty in the afternoon, and by seven thirty, we had not heard from him. Fortunately, he remembered where we wrote down our phone number in his bag and was able to call us. He was kilometers away, but we were able to find him and pick him up. After the third day, he made it home by getting off at the right stop. We celebrated!

Noel, son number two, at age nine, was more flexible. He continued playing cello and seemed happy and content to carry on with his normal activities. We entered him in the Eisteddfod, a national music competition at various levels according to age. He placed first in his level, which of course made us proud and would have made his teacher in Claremont, California, Louisa Miller, proud as well.

He continued with cello until he lost interest in high school. I realized this when he asked me if he could play guitar instead of cello. As a string player with hopes and expectations that at least one of our kids would carry on with the string tradition in the family, I emphatically said no! He showed promise on cello and had such a good foundation I thought it was just a passing fancy and his desire to be like his friends. He persisted, so when he was in his junior year of high school, we gave in and allowed him to take guitar lessons. I made sure he understood that guitarists were a dime a dozen and we would expect him to at least be the best!

When he began his higher education studies at our college, we assigned David Holmes to be his teacher. David was a Christian and a professional with extensive experience as a session player, and he was our only guitar teacher on staff. It proved to be the right combination, and Noel excelled at a rapid pace.

The guitar became his passion. At that time, Wesley Institute had only an accredited diploma in music, but he was able to gain acceptance with a scholarship to USC. I was proud to hear he was hailed as the most outstanding sight-reader at USC. Faculty and students alike wanted to know where he had done his previous studies to become such an outstanding musician. Following graduation from USC with a BA in studio guitar and a minor in philosophy, he returned to Sydney and taught at our college. He also recorded his first album, *Possible Worlds*, at the Sydney Opera House recording studio. A year later, he accepted a graduate/teaching scholarship at the University of North Texas, where he gained his master's in jazz guitar. It was also where he met his talented and lovely wife, Jiyoung. They have two gifted boys, Aiden and Toby.

Our daughter, Missy, at age four, adapted very quickly. She attended preschool and loved it but became tired of it after one day and announced she wouldn't be going back. It was no easy task to convince her to stay on the bus when leaving for school the next day. Marianna would put her on the bus, and she would immediately and repeatedly get right off. Finally, Marianna told the driver to close the door and take off, keeping her on board.

It's not hard to imagine the vast number of incidents that added to the culture shock we were all experiencing. There was the time Marianna was at the grocery store with her list and unable to find one item on it because every single thing had a different name or was not available in Australia. She remembers standing in an aisle sobbing, wondering how she would ever be able to prepare meals for the family.

So much had happened up to this point that I had not stopped to remind myself that I was going there to start a college, something I had never done before nor had any idea of where or how to begin. In the meantime, word got out that I was coming, and when prospective students began to inquire, they were told to just wait and David would soon be there and would answer all their questions.

My plan was to take at least the first six months to acclimatize to the new environment and familiarize myself with the New South Wales education system and establish some connections and meet people. I knew nothing of the Australian education systems, nor did I have any network or connections of any kind. I had no knowledge of the first steps in setting up programs in the fields we planned to offer. When people began to ask questions and I realized no one had answers, I just made them up on the spot. I wasn't sure if the answers were correct, but it became clear that I had to go on blind faith that they were.

I do have to say that our all-knowing Heavenly Father already knew we would find ourselves in a foreign land and that I would be starting a ministry and arts school of higher education. During the year before we left the United States, we found ourselves in the Bay Area visiting old friends who served on the staff with us in Bakersfield and Pomona, Don and Marilyn Anderson. We were also there to see Leighton Sheley, one of our fine baritone singers and actors in the Red Letter Edition. Leighton's mother, Vernita, is the founder of Highlands Christian Schools, which is part of the Church of the Highlands. Leighton chose to complete his internship under me in

Pomona in partial fulfillment of his degree requirements in music ministry at Bethany Bible College.

While we were visiting, I was able to spend some time with Mrs. Sheley, who kept giving me handouts and information on educational requirements for adequate facilities, fire regulations, human resource guidelines, and all the way through to accreditation standards and requirements. I was just being polite in taking all the material thinking I would probably never make use of it, but we packed all that material and took it with us to Australia. Little did I know at the time how beneficial that material would be to us.

Back in Sydney, a charming couple in the church invited us for dinner just for us to meet some people they thought would be good for us to know. We gladly accepted the invitation. I recall driving to Mosman, parking the car, entering their apartment building, and making our way to the fourth floor. The views from their apartment were spectacular. Their balcony was directly across from the famous Sydney Opera House, and the view of the Sydney Harbour was breathtaking.

I also recall sitting in a window seat and speaking with Lynne Williams that evening and was captivated by the conversation with her. Lynne worked in the music department at Wollongong University and had just finished a successful application for reaccreditation of the university's bachelor of music program and had just started a leave of absence for a year. She and her husband, John, lived in Wollongong, on the coast about an hour's drive south of Sydney.

Lynne asked many questions about what I was doing in Australia and why we came to Sydney. I was a little uncomfortable when attempting to answer some of her questions without having more knowledge of what was involved in starting a college.

That night on their drive back to Wollongong, Lynne said to her husband, John, "I don't think I'll be taking this year off; I have an idea I'll be helping David with setting up his college."

This incident drew my attention to the fact that God was affirming He was with me and answering prayer. The next day, I received a phone call from Lynne. She had been up all night drawing charts with lines, squares, and circles in an attempt to graphically illustrate the structure of what she understood me to say I had in mind for the college. She drove up to Sydney that same day, and we looked over the charts. It definitely helped clarify my concept of what I had in mind.

A few days later, I paid a visit to the Higher Education Board in Sydney and asked what the appropriate steps were for us to follow in order to set up a state-accredited private college. That was the first time I experienced receiving blunt Australian insults in a professional setting. I was all but laughed at and was told to start the enterprise and run it for at least ten years and, if it was still in operation, I could then address the standards necessary for state recognition. That answer was just not good enough for me. But I think they got tired of me asking, so I was finally given the guidelines necessary for us to get started with the process.

CHAPTER 13

Feast of Tabernacles

It was within the first year of living in Sydney and attending Christian Life Centre that we met a family who had just returned to Australia from the mission field in Zimbabwe. Gerald and Elizabeth Rowlands, with their two daughters, Kathy and Virginia, extended an invitation to our family for dinner one evening. It was at that time we learned about their ministry with the International Christian Embassy in Jerusalem. Gerald was a well-known missionary statesman, author, and teacher. They told us about the annual Christian celebration during Sukkot in Israel called the Feast of Tabernacles. I could just imagine the high-energy event with the elaborate costumes and integration of music, dance, and worship with magnificent staging. This annual event was sponsored by the Christian Embassy in Jerusalem.

As our friendship grew, we were delighted to receive an invitation to attend the Feast and for me to participate by playing violin in the orchestra. Although the Feast was a relatively new event during Sukkot, it had already established certain traditions.

As an educator, I sent a letter to the embassy expressing my appreciation for what they were doing, as well as thanking them for the invitation extended to Marianna and me to be part of the event. I felt the least I could do was include a critique of the event expressing my opinion of how we could improve each of the eight nights' productions. As it represented a unified front as Christians around the world, I felt it was critical that we should relate to the Israelis by building bridges with the Jewish people through excellence in the arts. My ideas were embraced, and I was invited to serve as the music director of the Feast for the following seventeen years.

The world's largest, most colorful, high-energy Christian event during the Jewish holiday, Sukkot, every year draws thousands of pilgrims from over one hundred nations to worship and celebrate Yeshua, the Messiah for the whole world. This epic event, known as the Feast of Tabernacles, is sponsored each year by the International Christian Embassy Jerusalem (ICEJ). The International Christian Embassy was founded in 1980 by evangelical Christians to express their support for the State of Israel and the Jewish people, specifically the Israeli government's enactment of the Jerusalem Law, and in protest of the closure of foreign embassies in Jerusalem but has since been restored.

During the years from 1986 to 2000 that I served as music director of the Feast, the embassy was directed by one of its founders, Dr. Johann Luckhoff, from 1980 to 2000. When I think back to those years, I marvel at the breadth of understanding and knowledge this man had of the vast multicultural sensitivities represented by those in attendance. He was able to adhere to the number of protocols required to transcend whatever barriers might have existed between the nations represented. Generally, the classical repertoire speaks to the hearts of the Jewish people and appeals to every culture I can think of around the world. Fortunately for me, my personal taste in music leans toward the classical genre. Much planning went into the selection of repertoire for each of the eight nights of presentations.

I had some of the most fulfilling experiences of my life working with Johann and like-minded artists. It was always a joy to work with great talent from so many countries. The Christian Embassy sponsored so many planeloads of Russian Jews, bringing them home to Israel to make *aliyah*. This influx of Russian immigrants significantly increased the number of Russians in my orchestra, especially the violin section. I couldn't help but notice how solemn the Russian musicians were during our rehearsals and felt the need to assure them they were safe and should not fear that they would be fired if they missed a note or made a mistake. I wanted them to feel at ease and secure and even enjoy our rehearsals, so after several hours of intensive rehearsing, I would attempt to break the atmosphere by speaking in my Donald Duck voice and then observe the big smiles that would come across their faces, exposing their sparkling gold teeth that practically blinded me!

The lineup of artists with whom I worked at the various feasts was indeed an enriching experience. It was heartwarming to work with the likes of violinist Serguei and his wife, Helena, prima ballerina assoluta; bass/baritone Jonathan Settel; worship leaders Claren McQueen and Roy Kendall; violist and baritone John Shuffle; and also many of our IICM students, administration, and faculty who also participated. Over the years, I was able to bring to the stage some world-renowned performing artists such as my nephew and trumpet virtuoso Ryan Anthony; the beautiful soprano and vocal tutor at Wesley Institute and formerly with the Sydney and English National Opera companies, Christa Leahmann; and composer and tenor Steve Fry.

The leadership group, on which I served, met for hours collaborating and discussing the repertoire that would best support the theme and subthemes for each night. This group was made up of the creative arts director of the Feast Randall Bane, now deceased but a brilliant mime. He was never short of ideas. There was Valerie Henry, whose choreography and dance movements were always so tasteful, graceful, and meaningful in lifting praises to God. Her soft personality, beauty, and gentleness yet self-confidence made her a strong leader. I loved working with Valerie; we were always on the same page.

When I first came to the Feast, Ramona Dicks was in charge of the choir. She was never short of original compositions and always had one ready at the drop of a hat. Her buoyant spirit and humor kept things moving in rehearsals.

There were musicians, singers, dancers, artists, and actors coming to Jerusalem from the four corners of the world to make this event come alive. There were so many highlights that come to mind through the years. One in particular was the night of the Hosanna Integrity recording with Paul Wilbur, *Jerusalem Arise*, held in the Jerusalem Convention Center. All songs on the recording, by the same name, *Jerusalem Arise*, were original songs and recorded live during the Feast.

In rehearsal that day with the orchestra and choir, one of the arrangements wasn't coming together. The producer and arranger, Paul Mills, explained that he did most of the arrangements on the plane coming over, so it was no wonder that there were places in the score that weren't tried and airtight. Unfortunately, we had run out of time in rehearsal, so he felt he had no choice but to cut the overture from the performance that night. I was disappointed because I thought it had been written so tastefully and set the atmosphere and tone for the worship and musical experience that would follow.

I asked if I could take the score to my room and work on it. I was sure I could repair the problem and make it work! The response was that, if I could rewrite the parts and make them super clear for the musicians and singers, we would take the time just before the performance to go through it once just to make sure it worked. If it worked, then it would be included. I was so glad I did that because it actually worked and worked very well! I genuinely felt it was an honor for me to have had an input in the overture. In the ending, I indicated a dynamic orchestral crescendo building to a strong choral entrance toward the end, making sure the singers blended perfectly, all shaping the same with wide-open mouths and on a totally matching open, dark, yet bright sound on the open vowel *ah*. This shaped a dramatic tonal cluster and created just the right balance of harmonic tension, setting the stage for the intense excitement in anticipation of what was to come next.

What made it so perfect for Marianna and me to spend a few weeks in Jerusalem every year is that, while I was conducting rehearsals preparing the musicians and singers for the Feast, Marianna would be spending time absorbing the culture and people and visiting the Israel Museum every year or archaeological digs. Her studies eventually led to her obtaining a master's degree in biblical studies through Hebrew University and Dr. Jim Fleming of Biblical Resources.

Most of the evening presentations were held in the Jerusalem Convention Center, but the opening night was an outdoor event at Qumran, on a hillside near the caves where the Dead Sea Scrolls were discovered and overlooking the Dead Sea reflecting the full moon. There were thousands of pilgrims from all over the world who enjoyed this spectacular setting while sitting on the ground or on folding chairs enjoying the drama, Israeli dance, and musical presentation while eating a Bedouin meal provided by the embassy and prepared by local residents. Each year, this event would set the tone and atmosphere for the Christian celebration of the Feast of Tabernacles.

Opening night of the Feast of Tabernacles at Qumran and the Dead Sea

Midweek there was usually a classical concert held at Christ Church just inside the Jaffa Gate in the Old City. This Anglican church, the oldest protestant church in the Middle East, was the venue for a special concert consisting primarily of classical works. The acoustics alone made it a highlight for those listening and performers alike. It was a pleasure and joy for me to have the freedom to basically perform on my Carlo Giuseppe Testore 1715 violin anything I desired as well as to conduct from a wide selection of classical orchestral repertoire. Working with members of the Feast orchestra during this event and every other night of the Feast was a real pleasure for me, the participants, and the audience.

I love Israel. Working with the Feast was not the only purpose for making the trips. I'll never forget the experience in 1993 of having the privilege and honor of performing a violin solo at the Zionist Congress in the breathtaking Chagall Room in the Knesset during a banquet with Prime Minister Yitzhak Rabin.

In recent years, Marianna and I have led a number of tours to Israel. Combining my trips to Israel to conduct Feasts, lead study tours, perform as violin soloist for special events, and attend the Zionist Congress and leadership summits total more than twenty visits to Israel.

CHAPTER 14

Off and Running

The Higher Education Board finally realized I wasn't going to go away and accepted my submission for the college to begin accreditation procedures. Still, they had no classification for such a school, and they said it had to be either a theological school or a school of the arts. I told them they had to consider creating a new category and get with the times because it was the future of higher education!

The regulation was the same then as it is now. To run an accredited course, the person teaching a subject would need to have at least one degree higher than the level they are teaching. To incorporate studying the Bible and the arts, I had to find highly accomplished Christian artists and individuals with degrees to teach Bible. The only resources I found for teaching the curriculum in theology or ministry were lay pastors in churches of various denominations in Australia. None of them had formal qualifications. Then it suddenly occurred to me that my wife, Marianna, held a degree in Bible! She often wondered if her degree would ever be useful. She was apprehensively delighted to find her place and be involved.

As inquiries came in, I found myself on the edge of darkness and taking that one step beyond many times by answering questions I didn't know the answers to. We needed space, so the church leased the tenth floor of a nearby building and partitioned the entire space with elegant dark wood-grained partitions according to an agreed design, giving adequate space for classrooms and offices for the church and school. I was able to hire a receptionist, Heather Ford, who was passionate about my vision and helped establish the tone, integrity, and image that the college enjoys to this day.

We had barely arrived in the country. It was only January, but with all the inquiries, we felt we had to set a starting date for the college and needed to think of a name.

A lot of inquiries were coming in from Southeast Asia and from other parts of the world as well—all by word of mouth. Whatever vision it was that had been conceived was already reaching out to the nations, so I felt the word *international* should be part of the name. I had discovered that *school* or *academy* in Australia would possibly infer that it was a primary or secondary school. Although *institute* could come across as too serious, it seemed to fit. At that point, we had part of the name International Institute.

The pastor in Townsville, Reverend David Cartledge, organized and produced our first tour itinerary in 1980. He strongly supported the Red Letter Edition and endorsed our ministry throughout the country. His son, David Jr., smitten by the Red Letter Edition and excited to have so many young people come to Townsville with whom he could relate, was an avid sound technician and enjoyed setting up and running the soundboard for the group. When the RLE departed from Townsville to complete the remaining itinerary in Australia, David Jr. traveled with the group and then on to the United States. He continued working with the group until the follow-up tour in Australia in 1982.

I often called Pastor Cartledge soon after we arrived in Sydney since he had already become a good friend from working together over the two years organizing the RLE tour. He would often encourage me to think outside the box and study the original Hebrew or Greek scripture to help gain a fuller understanding and depth of its meaning. I was drawn to Hebrews 10:24 as our motto for the institute and came up with "Let us consider how to spur one another on to love and noble creativity." We all felt the search for the name had come to a conclusion. It was to be called the International Institute for Creative Ministries (IICM).

It was now official; we named it the International Institute for Creative Ministries (IICM), complete with a logo designed by

Tony O'Connell, which was artistically duplicated in leather by Nita Brown. Its inaugural commencement date was June 1983. We began by offering a diploma course with all fifty-two full-time students taking the same subjects. We called it a foundation term. In the meantime, we continued to accept new applications for a more diversified curriculum planned for the following year.

As the days went by, I made promises I didn't know I could keep. I was desperate. I quickly learned that I couldn't stay if I didn't pray. My dependency on God increased. One day, I had a call from a prospective student who wanted to major in flute and asked if we had an advanced flute teacher. We didn't; but my reply to this prospective student was, yes, we would have one for her. I felt a lot of pressure at that moment, so I spoke with my receptionist and requested all calls be held and for any visitors to please wait as I was going to pray for God to send us a flute teacher and did not want to be disturbed. I just began to pray, and my phone rang, which I had to admit annoyed me. Heather, my receptionist on the line, announced she had a flute teacher on the phone and requested to speak with me. I accepted the call!

The voice on the other end of the line went something like this, "Hello, I'm one of the principal flute players in the Sydney Symphony. I heard about the Christian college you're starting and was wondering if you needed a flute teacher."

God's timing to this day never ceases to amaze me.

The institute was considered to be well and truly launched by this time. There were just too many incidents and events that we could call luck or just a coincidence. We would have to be blind to categorize any of them other than miracles and clear signs God was making straight the crooked roads ahead for us. Whenever I needed help, there was always someone there to help me or fulfill whatever needed to be done.

One of the early projects I launched was to create a media presentation similar to a documentary format that told the story of how the institute was birthed. This was an essential tool we used to promote our institute. The narration and soundtrack for this production were crucial in order to create the desired feel, image, atmosphere, and credibility. I felt we needed a professional voice to do the narration, so I listened to some of the more popular radio stations in Sydney and identified a voice that I thought would be perfect for the production. It was the voice of Grant Goldman. When we contacted him, I described what we wanted him to do. He somehow caught the excitement of my vision and not only said he would love to do it but insisted on doing it pro bono as his contribution to the institute.

When he came to the tenth floor to make the voice-over recording, he was concerned about how he would know when to pause and when to resume reading. We had the slide presentation set up, which he would watch in order to match the tone of his voice to the visual.

I said, "No problem, just watch me."

I stood in front of him and conducted as if he was an orchestra and gave him every cue when to come in and when to pause. I even used my conductor's baton. He then knew how fast or slow to pace the narration, including dynamics, inflection, and mood. It was great fun working with such a professional. It was recorded with perfection and in one take!

I've always said, "I'm easy to please…with perfection!"

Once the media production was complete, we sent out invitations to a formal dinner to be held in the ballroom of the Sydney Hilton Hotel. Among the guests, we invited to attend was the world-famous Australian artist Pro Hart. His name is Kevin Hart; but when he worked in the mines in Broken Hill, his workmates nicknamed him Pro, short for professor. He never got bored in his spare time because he was always drawing or painting something and anything. He would paint on sticks, pieces of scrap paper, napkins, and the back of his tinplate or whatever he could find.

His favorite subjects to paint at first were insects and stick figures. His charcoal drawings of dragonflies hang in the White House and in palaces around the world. He painted ants all over his Rolls-Royce. He was a free spirit and dared to be different. He had his favorite subjects to paint. Whether it was a dragonfly or a field of flowers created by cannon shots of various paint colors on a canvas, his art takes on various styles that are easily recognizable and define different periods in his painting style based on the subject matter and medium.

His last period before he passed away was painting flowers and bouquets. His daughter lost an infant child from cot death. Flowers were delivered to their compound, and he isolated himself to grieve the loss of a grandchild and couldn't help but paint the bouquet of flowers that he kept looking at that had been delivered to his studio. There have been hundreds of copies of that same painting sold to raise money for research of cot death.

Pro and his wife, Raylene, flew in from Broken Hill, New South Wales, at their own expense to honor the work we were about to launch.

When I asked him if he would be willing to speak and endorse the vision, he said, "I paint. I don't speak."

I then got an idea. I asked him if he would be willing for me to interview him, and he agreed without hesitation. Together with our kids, Marianna and I went to see them in their hotel the day before the banquet.

It was there when Dietrich (at age eleven) said to Mr. Hart, "I can draw ants better than you."

Pro was more than gracious. He folded the napkin upon which Dietrich had made his drawing and put it in his pocket and said, "Because it's so good, I'm going to save this!"

The formal evening in the grand ballroom came and was considered to be a huge success. It appeared that every one of our guests left with excitement and eagerness to tell their friends about IICM. In addition, we acquired our first mailing list!

Through this occasion, I was able to meet the famous Australian television personalities Dawn Lake and Bobby Limb. Through the years, they became special friends and major donors to the institute.

By this time, I was gradually catching on to the Australian mindset and Aussie way of doing things. However, I couldn't accept the lack of emphasis on Easter by the churches in Sydney and really the whole country. They referred to Easter as the "long weekend." It was an opportunity to go camping or just have a mini holiday. Since the Easter story is one that every Christian should stand on the highest mountain and shout the loudest that Jesus is alive, I wanted to at least make a dent in the culture of the city by involving every Christian from every church to join in creating a massive production, which we would produce at the new ten-thousand-seat Sydney Entertainment Centre.

The production, which we called *Easter Alive,* was emceed by Dawn Lake and Bobby Limb and featured a ninety-piece symphony orchestra and a three-hundred-voice choir. Other well-known Australian artists were featured that night for the nearly ten thousand enthusiastic Sydneysiders in the audience.

One year, when visiting friends and relatives we had in the United States, we attended the Pageant of the Masters in Laguna Beach, California. Each year, Leonardo da Vinci's *The Last Supper* painting is the finale of Pageant of the Masters or "living paintings" production. It is an annual event and has grown from eight performances in 1933 to fifty-six shows today.

My desire was to reproduce this famous scene in our *Easter Alive* productions. Immediately following the performance, I made my way to the office around back hoping to meet the producers. Fortunately, I found them and was able to meet the director as well. They were quite cordial when they heard that I was from Australia. When I asked if I could go backstage and take measurements of their Last Supper table and backdrop so we might construct and reproduce the same scene in Sydney as part of our *Easter Alive* productions, they were more than accommodating.

One of the gentlemen took me backstage and actually helped me measure the table and props and even allowed me to take photos. All I can say is that it worked. I recall being so amazed that the table was only ten inches wide but built on a slant to give the illusion of being much bigger. Marianna was successful at recreating the plates and cups on a slant with her skills in paper sculpture. The entire scene was an optical illusion. Volunteers designed and sewed the wardrobe worn by the disciples.

Of course, the DaVinci painting is nothing like what it was like during the first century. It was historically a triclinium with everyone at a three-sided table reclining on a mat according to rank.

Sometimes I think DaVinci must have instructed the disciples to all stand on one side of the table to get everyone in the picture. In our *Easter Alive* productions, the living portrait started dimly lit. As the music to the "Communion Song" began, the lights gradually came up; and the disciples would come alive and, with slow movements, reenact their part, breaking bread and drinking the wine. At the end of the song, the players would slowly resume their original positions and freeze till the lights were fully dimmed out. One could call it the dream scene.

Leonardo da Vinci—Last Supper—Living Portrait—Easter Alive 1985

There were three more *Easter Alive* productions that were held in other venues in the years following.

CHAPTER 15

Too Stubborn to Quit

Our greatest weakness lies in giving up. The most certain way to succeed is always to just try one more time.
—Thomas Edison

As the institute continued to grow and develop, more students created a need for more staff. More staff created a need for more money, and miraculously it all seemed to be coming together. Although we kept saying "One more year," it was just too exciting to leave. I have to admit that one of the reasons we kept staying was because I was too stubborn to quit. As I met with Dr. Moyes, it became clear that God was not finished with us in Australia. When God closes doors, He opens others. All I was able to do was go through the doors opened to us.

In the meantime, the institute was flourishing. Students were applying from all over the world; and I found myself writing curriculum, best practices, and procedures to comply with New South Wales and federal government regulations, which had never entered my mind that I would ever be doing. Many times, I wondered why I was chosen to head up this institute. The only thing I had was a vision and determination to fulfill that which I was called to do. It all seemed so inconceivable that I would find myself in such a position in a foreign land. Sometimes it was anything but pleasant dealing with seemingly insurmountable obstacles, criticism, and harsh comments that Americans weren't needed to be there for such a purpose or any purpose for that matter.

When things looked bleak, I genuinely wanted to say I did my best and gave it my best shot and just leave. But although I wanted to quit, I was too determined to make it work regardless of how things looked in the natural. Since high school, I tried to base my decisions on "Only one life, 'twill soon be past. Only what's done for Christ will last." When opposition and crushing criticism came, I kept my focus on why I was doing all this, and all I could do was to keep going. Many times, I was reminded of the words of Churchill, "We must press on regardless." We depended on God to not only lead us but show us how to achieve every task along the way as well.

When we agreed to make the move to Sydney, Marianna and I made a two-year commitment to the church (CLC), and the church made a two-year commitment to us of financial support. By the end of the second year, the institute had reached a level of development I never thought was possible in such a short time. It was simply all too exciting to leave at that point, so we kept saying "One more year." After twenty-eight years, we found ourselves still there!

Soon into the 1985 academic year, we received notice that the landlord of the buildings in Darlinghurst we were leasing for church and school was breaking our lease and we had to vacate both buildings in a matter of weeks. We had only days to find alternate venues for both the church and school. We didn't want to ever find ourselves in this situation again, so we were not looking for something to lease but for something to purchase. We did find a warehouse in Waterloo for sale. It would have to have a new roof and a new floor, but it was something to work with. We could pay it off and not have rent to worry about.

I discovered that donations to a church building fund were not tax deductible, but they were for a school. Having sought legal counsel, we established that, since the principal use of the building would be used primarily as a school, it would be legitimate to raise money for such a purpose and let donors know it would be tax deductible. As the legal director of the institute, I was the one called upon to sign the loan documents at the state bank in purchasing the warehouse in Waterloo. I was part of the committee that met to establish the design of the renovations in considering the needs of both the school and the church.

While it was being renovated, the church met at the Clancy Auditorium at the University of New South Wales. Although the renovations included space for the institute, it wasn't possible for it to be ready in time for the start of the coming new semester.

Meanwhile, the institute continued to flourish and was gaining attention throughout Australia and around the world, especially in Southeast Asia.

Again God had to come through in the eleventh hour, and my faith was tested. One week before school started, the Sisters of Charity heard we were "homeless" and offered their convent facility in Arncliffe for us to use for the institute until we could find a permanent campus of our own. Although it had been a boys' school in the past, it had been vacant for a number of years and vandalized numerous times, leaving it in shambles. Believe me, you had to be a real visionary to imagine it could be cleaned up and usable for any purpose, let alone an up-and-coming prestigious and elite college of the arts and ministry.

Campus cleanup

Our head student that year miraculously organized donations of paint and a crew of students to come in to clean and paint. We had to accept the colors that were donated, which were cobalt blue and hot pink! There was broken glass on the floors from rocks being thrown through windows, dead rats on the floor in several rooms, dust and debris, and years of neglect. Within a day, the entire complex was painted and cleaned, and most repairs were completed, ready for school to commence. Good job, Michael Newton-Brown and students!

Everything happened so fast that I failed to show adequate consideration for the community of nuns who lived there. There was the sweet and kind Sister Imelda, who was always gracious and enjoyed our presence in the convent bringing life once again within its walls. Then there was Sister Frances, the resident authority, most likely the Mother Superior of the convent whom we affectionately referred to as the gestapo. I met with her almost daily. She seemed displeased with us being there; and I think, in some ways, she regretted allowing us to use the facility.

Actually it was just a matter of asking permission and clearing with her what we wanted to do that made life a lot easier and much more tolerable for us all. As long as we acknowledged her authority, we got along just fine for the most part. Whenever she became annoyed with something one of our students said or did or whenever the students ventured off into a space within the convent where they shouldn't have, she would find me and, through her body language, demand to speak with me immediately right then and there. This became awkward at times, especially when I would be teaching a class. I felt as if I was in trouble so much of the time.

In spite of any restrictions placed upon us at the convent, it was God's provision of space and served us quite well. I was fortunate to have qualified, supportive, and committed staff who understood the vision and supported me. Kim Doust was my personal assistant—highly organized, the college bursar, and a gifted musician as well. It was actually fun deciding the best footprint by assigning what would be the best spaces for the various departments and classes including administration. The nuns' quarters on the second floor were small cubicles without doors or full walls. We turned them into teachers' and administrative staff's offices. There was a large space downstairs that was most likely a gymnasium at one time that became an amazing dance studio. We had to find someone to repair the holes in the floor. I think it was Willie Schmidt, Marianna's brother, who did the repairs and served as our college dean for a number of years. We then placed vinyl-linoleum-type covering specifically made for dance studios over the floor's surface. This was made possible by a generous donation from Bobby Limb, a prominent celebrity in Australia.

The years in the convent in Arncliffe were happy years.

IICM Graduation held at Christian Life Center, Waterloo 1986

Old Drummoyne Boys High School—New home for Wesley Institute

Since joining the CLC staff, I had been having weekly one-on-one meetings with Frank Houston, whom we all affectionately referred to as the bishop. So many changes happening so quickly. To add to the whirlwind of these changes, Marianna and I were about to leave for Israel to lead a study tour; so in my last one-on-one meeting with the bishop before our trip to Israel, I reported the results of my research of possible future venues for the institute. There were a number of potential options included in my report. We were given a warm invitation to partner with YWAM in Canberra, but it meant relocating outside Sydney. I personally was not in favor of relocating that far from Sydney as most of our Australian industry professional, casual, and part-time performing arts faculty were based in Sydney. I had also met with Rev. Dr. Gordon Moyes, who seemed interested in partnering with us but insisted there be a meeting with Frank Houston before it would be considered. He said he had ideas he would only discuss with the senior pastor of CLC.

When Frank heard that, his response was, "That sounds like the miracle we've been praying for!"

He assured me he would arrange a meeting with Gordon Moyes for a time soon after my return from Israel. It was at that time I had just taken a tour of the warehouse being renovated for the church and school. I was perplexed when I couldn't help but notice that what the workers were building was not according to the plans I was part of designing. For example, the art room had been designed to have ample natural light, and I was told that the space was not going to be used as an art studio but was now going to be the creche for the church. There was no longer a choir room. Other classrooms and institute offices were no longer included in the plan.

I was confused and finding it hard to understand what was going on. I just figured the bishop was believing God for a miracle to provide IICM with its own space. I immediately thought of how we would get around the tax department with the fact that we were registered as building a school and, in fact, it was not going to be a school at all. With the frantic and busy time for everyone in the church and institute staff, it was not a surprise that the weekly meetings I had been having with the bishop were put on hold. I brushed my paranoia aside and could only think of the meeting with Frank Houston and Gordon Moyes upon my return from Israel. We then took off for our study tour, and throughout that trip, I was so excited I could hardly contain myself with a feeling of tremendous satisfaction that I had possibly achieved something historic for the kingdom.

Little did we know what was about to happen to us next. There was, in fact, a meeting upon our return that included Marianna and the ministry team of the church. Not only was there no room for the institute in the plans for the relocation of the church in Waterloo, but we were also actually asked to leave the church! When I asked what happened with the plan to meet with Gordon Moyes, Frank didn't seem to remember anything about that.

When we first arrived in Sydney and started to work for the church, we were provided with a car, a Commodore SLE. It was used but a nice car, and we were grateful. By this point in time, it was in need of major repairs and seriously needed to be replaced, so I traded it in for a new Mitsubishi. I was able to make monthly payments with financing over a period of twenty-four months. I had one car payment left to make before it was paid off when a representative of the church came to our home and said he was there to pick up my car, claiming it belonged to the church. He asked for the key. I gave it to him, and he drove off in it.

We had just received notice that our power was being shut off by the electric company claiming it was in the name of the church. We also received notice that our telephone was going to be disconnected for the same reason. The lease of the house we were living in was in the name of the church as well. We can look back and see that God had His hand on us in a powerful way. We thought we were in a canoe without a paddle, but God took over.

I really wanted to purchase our return flights to the United States but didn't have the resources. I searched the employment section of the *Sydney Morning Herald* and local newspapers for several days looking for teaching positions, but in every case, I was told I was overqualified. A wave of discouragement came over me for days. At the same time, I would receive phone calls and unannounced and unexpected visitors coming to our door telling me how terrible I was for not leaving sooner because I was causing Frank Houston to feel stressed.

About that time, we were contacted by another pastor in Sydney, Pastor Tony Hallo. I had met him previously on occasion but really didn't know him that well. He was the pastor of the Petersham Assembly of God Church. He had heard what happened to us and made contact to let me know someone in his church was loaning us a car for as long as we needed it. A representative of the church came to our house and handed me an envelope and said it was from the church with a message from the pastor saying we must accept it as coming from the Lord and God's provision. I opened it after the messenger left. It was the exact amount we needed to keep our utilities on and our house lease transferred to our name with the bond required. As far as we were concerned, Pastor Tony Hallo was the person of Jesus in the flesh to us at that time.

Naturally, Marianna and I were concerned about what impact the series of recent events would have on our children. It had been too often I observed the effects of parents being treated uncaringly by the church, resulting in bitterness in the hearts of their children. It's like the church is sometimes guilty of shooting the wounded on the battlefield as opposed to nurturing and caring for them.

We were feeling rather confident that it would only be another year or two before leaving Australia anyway and returning to the United States. Our oldest child, Dietrich, never adapted to Australia. A serious and genuine invitation from some very close friends was extended for him to live with them, Donna and Oogie Schmitt, in South Pasadena, California, until we returned. He was only sixteen, but his need to connect with his academic work and spiritual growth outweighed our desire for him to remain in Australia with us. We felt compelled to allow him to go.

I'll never forget that day when I held Marianna in my arms, sobbing as we stood on that hill on the southeast end of the campus at the convent in Arncliffe watching his plane pass overhead winging our son back to the United States separating us for what we thought was to be a short time but still aching.

I was reminded of my mother telling me how heartbroken my grandmother was when she left home at the age of sixteen. I was sixteen when I left home to attend Canyonville Bible Academy in Oregon, and it broke my mother's heart to see me go. My plan was to return after high school graduation and live at home with my parents while attending college, but my mother passed away unexpectedly from a failed heart operation to open a valve partially closed from having scarlet fever when she was a child. I was sixteen at the time of her death. Our oldest grandchild was sixteen when her mother, our daughter-in-law, passed away from a pulmonary embolism that formed as a result of a sprained ankle. (I guess sixteen isn't always so sweet!)

Once again, news came that the institute would have to relocate, this time due to the convent being sold. We found ourselves again at the threshold of witnessing God's provision. I just needed to find out what that was. For whatever reason, the sponsoring church, upon renovating the factory in Waterloo, left no space for the institute, all the more reason to assume the convent was God's provision for us at the time.

By this time, with all that had transpired, I thought surely it must have been the time to leave and move back to the United States. There was still that small voice telling me my work in Australia was not finished. I submitted a bid to purchase the convent property myself just in case that was what God wanted me to do. My bid was four times less than what the reserve was on the property, but if my bid had been accepted, I had no idea what lending agency would lend me $3 million to purchase it.

The year was 1989; and the institute was in its sixth year and had grown exponentially and, by that time, was recognized as a quality higher education provider of accredited diploma and certificate courses. Throughout the years since opening the institute, the promotional and advertising media we had been using to promote our courses and special events, such as *Easter Alive* and other productions, was through television and radio. The largest radio station in Sydney was 2GB, owned by Wesley Mission. The *Sunday Night Live* radio broadcast was hosted by the mission's superintendent, Rev. Dr. Gordon Moyes. He also hosted a weekly television program, *Turn*

'Round Australia. Our student housing facility in Enfield, Pinnaroo, was also leased from Wesley Mission.

When I stopped to think about it, the link with Wesley Mission had been there almost since the beginning. Dr. Moyes was always willing to promote our institute on television and radio and was excited that such a college existed in Australia. I admired him as an author, a great speaker, a preacher, a man of God, and an entrepreneur.

I was fascinated to hear his story of when he and his wife, Beverley, were having dinner in the revolving restaurant in the Centrepoint Tower. While sitting at their table next to the window, Dr. and Mrs. Moyes looked down at Wesley Mission next to it buried among so many skyscrapers.

He then said to Beverley, "We are not being good stewards of the airspace God has given us."

He then designed a magnificent conference center with five levels of underground parking and more than forty levels above ground. The cost was greater than a $300-million project and offered ninety-nine-year leases to companies that would occupy the levels the Mission didn't need and wasn't planning to use, which financially enabled the Mission to move into the new Wesley Centre debt-free.

Wesley Mission is a church that started as a mission in 1812 feeding the hungry, housing the homeless, and clothing the poor. It began before the formation of the Australian government. Dr. Moyes was a visionary, and under his leadership, over five hundred centers were established under the auspices of the Mission.

It sometimes pains me to think how different things would have turned out had Gordon Moyes and Frank Houston, two visionaries, actually met together to consider what God might have in store by working together. To imagine what could have been gave me unspeakable joy. For whatever reason, while I was on tour in Israel, Frank canceled the meeting and decided he no longer had a desire for CLC to be associated with Wesley Mission or the institute. I never knew why.

I thought surely this would be my cue to exit and return to the United States with my family. After all, it was 1989, and we had six good years of watching how God impacted the lives of our students and knowing we had planted seeds that would one day reap a harvest.

We had clearly worked hard living out the motto of "Only what's done for Christ will last." By faith, we had to leave the work we had done in God's hands and trust that the work we had started would *last* in the hearts and lives of our students.

While we were working toward preparing for our move back to the United States, Dr. Moyes called me and said he heard what happened to us but, if I found myself in a pioneering mood again, to come and see him and discuss the possibility of starting another school under the umbrella of Wesley Mission. I really was not interested. Besides, Marianna and I were both tired and wounded beyond measure. Things happened that we could not understand. Why were we given notice that our utilities in our home were going to be shut off? Why did a representative of CLC come to our house and drive off with my car? All we knew was we had to forgive and allow God to carry us because it was even hard to breathe at that point. I also realized we didn't have enough money to purchase plane tickets for the family to return to the United States, much less the cost of moving. It was indeed a time of testing. Marianna and I decided, in the meantime, we would pay Dr. Moyes a visit and at least hear what he had to say.

I have to admit that part of why we were still there was because I was too stubborn to quit. As I met with Dr. Moyes, it became clear that God was not finished with us in Australia. When God closes doors, He opens others. All I was able to do was go through the doors opened to us.

Open Day on the Drummoyne campus

CHAPTER 16

A Place of Beginning Again

Try not to become a person of success, but rather try to become a person of value.
—Albert Einstein

The resources of Wesley Mission were considerably greater than that of Christian Life Centre. If I were to begin again, my plan would be to take the time to set up the infrastructure of the new college and announce the start date to be at least six months from that time. However, almost immediately, we became aware that all but a couple of students and one staff member were left without a college to attend at CLC. There we were toward the end of the academic year, and CLC pronounced IICM *closed*. Some students were from other countries and on student visas. They pleaded for us to open the new college sooner rather than later so they could transfer to the new college and avoid deportation. There were thirteen students due to graduate in just a few weeks, so Wesley Mission provided an elaborate graduation ceremony and reception for them. They also honored the contracts of all teachers and staff and credited each student's account with the same balance they had at IICM even if they had already paid in full for the remainder of the year—another amazing act of generous support of Wesley Mission.

We were stunned at the extravagant generosity of the Mission. With the resources provided by the Mission, we soon became a well-oiled machine and grew exponentially. The Department of Higher Education was sympathetic to our change and considered it to be the same college they had accredited as we had continued with the same administration, students, and staff. It soon offered fully accredited bachelor's and postgraduate degrees recognized by the federal and state governments. At this time, it was known as Creative Ministries International (CMI).

We were functioning well in the new Wesley Centre, but the same space was also a greatly sought-after space in the heart of the city for conferences. In fact, it soon became an issue. Even though students had paid fees, if a corporate client requested a room that was being used as a classroom, the center management would cancel the class in favor of the client's request to use the room. Since the institute did not pay rent, the decision was easy because the mission's conference center needed the revenue to help balance its budget. Needless to say, this did not go over too well with the students. It was evident the college needed its own campus. About a year later, a search committee identified the former Drummoyne Boys' High School as a suitable campus for the institute.

As the school became more well-known internationally as a government-recognized higher education provider to which student visas could be granted, the name Creative Ministries International became problematic. One of the foreign consulates thought we were called Creative Mini-Strips International. There was actually nothing in the name that inferred it was an education provider or what product it offered, so at the time of the move to Drummoyne, it was decided that we would henceforth be called Wesley Institute for Ministry and the Arts. After all, John and Charles Wesley both exemplified the ethos of our vision.

Meanwhile, on another front and personal level, Marianna and I had been waiting to purchase a home in Sydney and waited until we knew where the institute would ultimately be located so we could find a house closer to the campus to avoid a long commute, such as the one we had to endure driving to and from the convent in Arncliffe from our home in Artarmon. I did not do well in rush traffic to and from Arncliffe every day and felt there was so much wasted time spent on the road when I could be engaged in my work.

Overseas residents were given an extension of four years to reinvest in the purchase of another home to avoid capital gains tax as opposed to the normal two-year period in the United States. Time passed so quickly, and we found ourselves in the fourth year after selling our home in Upland in Southern California. We were now facing the deadline to purchase another home to avoid capital gains.

During the years leading up to this time, whenever we had the occasion to set sail on the Sydney Harbour, we couldn't help but observe the thousands of homes around the harbor that would undoubtedly have spectacular views of the most beautiful harbor in the world.

I would say to God, *With all the amazing homes with these breathtaking views, I would like to have just 'one' of them.*

Without knowing where the campus would be, we were compelled to purchase something regardless of where it was, so we found a home in Drummoyne with a lovely view of Sydney Harbour, the city skyline, the Harbour Bridge, and North Sydney. We attended the auction, and miraculously our bid was the highest one. It was later that year the Mission discovered and purchased Drummoyne Boys' High School. I don't think it was a coincidence that we just happened to have purchased a home in Drummoyne. God was guiding us without a doubt. After moving into our new home in Drummoyne and when we were operating on our new campus, I had a mere two-minute commute to work—yet another miracle.

CHAPTER 17

Extending the Borders

The college grew, and more degrees were added to the curriculum. As my networking and knowledge of higher education administration increased, it became apparent that the institute filled a unique niche market in Australia and possibly the world. Economically it was critical that the institute grows in student numbers, so I began to think beyond the borders of Australia. I knew of a number of Christian colleges in the United States but none that offered the unique integration of theology and the arts as Wesley Institute. I set my sights on presenting my vision of a studies-abroad program to as many Christian colleges in the United States as possible, so I set up an itinerary to make my presentation of an Australian studies-abroad program to eighteen Christian colleges across the United States.

I was impressed with the warm welcome and hospitality of each of the colleges and universities where I visited and made my presentation. Primarily it was the president or the provost with whom I would meet initially but sometimes I was invited to speak at a luncheon or dinner either to a group of staff members designated by the president to attend or to anyone interested in hearing about a unique studies-abroad opportunity for their students.

When meeting with the provost of Azusa Pacific University, I heard about the Council of Christian Colleges and Universities (CCCU) based in Washington, DC. I learned of their support of Christian higher education as well as their annual conferences. Upon my return to Sydney, I applied to the institute board to attend the next presidents' conference the following year, which was held in

Washington, DC. My application was successful, and by attending the conference, I soon realized the importance of networking with other college presidents. It forged relationships that continue to this day.

It was at this conference I became so passionate to create a studies-abroad program in Australia based at our institute. The CCCU was already offering a significant number of studies-abroad programs all over the world, but I wanted to add an Australian program to the list of studies-abroad options for American students drawing from all the Christian colleges in the United States. A number of colleagues felt that the Australian culture was too similar to the United States and wouldn't offer a wide-enough cultural difference to qualify as a studies-abroad program. Having lived in Australia for almost thirty years and becoming an Australian citizen, I was certain, although in some cases admittedly some differences were more subtle than others, the cultural and mindset differences were vast.

By the time I made the submission and presentation at a subsequent presidents' conference, I was evidently so persuasive that the CCCU deemed Wesley's studies-abroad program to be a separate, stand-alone program under their banner but without the curriculum and teaching staff being appointed by the CCCU with oversight over it. They were convinced I was more than capable of running the program in-house. We set a cap of fifty US students for the Australia Study Centre (ASC) per semester to maintain a healthy ratio of Australian and overseas students. The program ran successfully for another decade after my retirement from the institute, led by a very capable young woman from the US, Kimberly Spragg.

As the institute grew and developed, it became clear that it was taking its place in the arena of excellence in higher education in Australia and around the world. At the same time, I came to realize that it really should be a level playing field in terms of government recognition and support, which clearly it was not. For example, there were some incidences when we would have an outstanding Australian citizen apply who had been accepted only to discover that they hadn't shown up for orientation on the first day of the semester. When investigating, we found out that the applicant chose a state university because it offered Austudy (a government loan to cover fees) and we did not.

After the persistent lobbying of parliament and government leaders, the New South Wales higher education and the federal government departments soon had to make it clear that any higher education provider that gained accreditation for their courses was at the same standard as any college or university with the same accreditation. After years of lobbying for parliament to recognize our institute on the same level as state universities for its students to be eligible for the same privileges and government support, we finally were able to offer Austudy; but for private providers, it was called FEE-HELP.

In order for students to apply and receive FEE-HELP, they must be enrolled in an accredited degree program and apply for government funding to pay for each unit individually that appears on the list of approved subjects for their specific degree. In order for each unit to be approved, the institute was required to submit a thorough rationale for why that subject was required to be taken for a particular degree, along with extensive documentation of what was required for successful completion of the unit and how it would be taught along with the qualifications of the instructor teaching it. This must be done a minimum of eighteen months prior to the commencement of the unit.

All units required for our accredited degrees were accepted at the time of gaining FEE-HELP, but new units subsequently introduced in any accredited degree program had to be submitted separately.

I believe that having the experience of being on a choir tour is of great value in a student's education, and I had a desire for such an experience to be included in the education of a music graduate of WI. When writing the submission to the Department of Higher Education, I made a case for a choir tour to Europe to be a legitimate elective unit for inclusion in the music degree curriculum, so I called it Cultural Enrichment through Performance. This was ultimately accepted and included in the approved curricula for the following year. Since FEE-HELP covered the costs, no one was left behind, and it brought the music department of WI to a whole new level. I observed that consequently every member became highly motivated to work hard in rehearsals and do their very best. It was a life-changing, uplifting experience.

CHAPTER 18

And the Winner Is...

Among the many unique aspects of Wesley Institute (WI) was that, every music major, regardless of their major instrument—studying violin, voice, drums, trumpet, or whatever—was required to study voice and sing in the choir. Ever since I became passionate about the human voice and studied it seriously for many years, I was convinced that every music student should gain knowledge of the voice and engage in a study of working within an ensemble setting. The voice is the instrument God gave everyone at birth. To add skill to this gift develops discipline and community, which every musician needs to succeed in the field. Furthermore, it facilitates ear training and listening skills and increases a greater sense of pitch, dynamic control, and discipline in all the complexities of an ensemble, including matching the quality of vowel formation and following the conductor.

After I led so many performance tours with groups from church and school, it was apparent that the experience had a deep impact on every participant. I was convinced that, without exception, every tour member grew and matured artistically and personally from such an experience. I had always wanted to take a performance group on tour from the Institute to Europe and enter them in a competition. So I set out to include this tour in the curriculum.

It was 2007. I announced that, in the following year, I was going to enter the choir in the International Summa Cum Laude Choral Festival competition in Vienna, Austria, as well as a concert tour of the music capitals of Europe, and it would all be covered under FEE-HELP. Every member of the choir was more than excited. The atmosphere of our rehearsals changed and became much more serious and focused, which was the desired objective. The students were motivated to work hard.

Wesley Institute Choir live from the Sydney Opera House
Easter morning sunrise national Broadcast—2008

Institute Choir European Tour—Santa Maria Majore—Rome 2007

David and Marianna—Graduation Day for Wesley Institute
theology students held at the University of Sydney

Was I dreaming? How awesome and thrilling an experience it was for our choir to tour through Italy, France, Germany, and Austria performing mostly in cathedrals, such as the famous Basilica di Santa Maria Maggiore in Rome. It was built in the mid-fourth century under the orders of the pope. The acoustics in these places helped to form a concept and mental image of the ultimate blend that the beauty of human voices could produce. One of the cathedrals just outside Florence, Italy, had acoustics with a seven-second delay. When I recall the sound of my choir in that place, I sometimes still get goosebumps.

The day came for the competition. There were too many groups to remember all of them; but there were choirs, orchestras, and chamber groups from the United States, Ukraine, Iraq, Moldova, New Zealand, Brazil, China, and many other countries. Every member of every group came full of hope that they would gain the recognition of placing within the top four. Whichever choir won first place would have the honor of giving a performance in the gala concert on the final night of the festival in the beautiful and famous Golden Hall of the Wiener Musikverein, the home of the Vienna Philharmonic.

After all the choirs and orchestras performed for the judges, everyone gathered in the concert hall to hear the announcement of where each group had placed. I was honestly praying I would not be embarrassed if my group had not even placed in the top four. I knew how hard each member worked, and I knew how hard I worked. Everyone's emotions were running high. When the announcer announced fourth place, it was not Wesley Institute! I didn't know if I should be relieved of the fear that we hadn't even placed at all. Then the third-place winner was announced, and the crowd went wild. But again it was not Wesley Institute.

This was the point when I thought, *Oh no, we didn't even place.*

Then it was announced that the boys' choir from Arizona had won second place. It was definitely accurate; they were truly excellent! But at that point, my heart sank thinking we had failed to even place in the top four. What was I going to tell the administration back home and Neil McEwan from the conservatorium, who spent so much time coaching the group in the skills of blending and professionalism?

Upon receiving the guidelines for preparing for this competition, we knew we had to prepare a certain set repertoire, a piece of our choosing composed by an indigenous composer and pieces written in French, German, Italian, English, and Russian. Recordings were available from which the conductor could study and gain an idea and concept of the style of each piece. A piece required of every group was an original composition in German composed by a local Austrian composer, W. Wagner, entitled "dir," to which there was no recording. It was strategically selected to test the director's ability to interpret the style and textual context.

Having studied in Austria some years earlier, I could still remember a fair amount of German. The text was basically a love letter from a gentleman written to his girlfriend, revealing his feelings and his heart toward her. I believed it was rare for a German gentleman to allow himself to be vulnerable in expressing his true feelings so openly in a letter like that, so I trained the choir to exaggerate the display of passion that the man must have had for the girl to write a letter like that. I made sure the choir understood the importance of exuding great passion and intense emotion when telling the story in song.

Then the announcer gave a long introduction about the choir that had won first place and, in particular, their interpretation of "dir." When he said "And the winner is Wesley Institute," the crowd went nuts, and you would have thought the members of my choir had won a gold medal at the Olympics or came in first place in the Kentucky Derby! It was encouraging to hear comments from the judges, things such as "The Wesley Institute choir had a fresh sound," "The choir demonstrated versatility in the various styles," and "Their interpretation of 'dir' showed musical maturity and insight."

If I could gather together all the members of that choir, I would tell them how much that experience has meant to me. I still hear from a number of students who also recall it being a significant event in their lives. It was significantly a build-up and climax of all that had gone on before. It was certainly the most memorable.

To God be the glory!

CHAPTER 19

International Educator of the Year

When Dr. Michael Whyte, provost of Azusa Pacific University, was the guest speaker at the graduation ceremony of Wesley Institute in 2009, he began by making a special presentation and asked me, "How many people were at Wesley Institute when you arrived?"

I was a little nonplussed and said none, and then Michael was the one taken aback. You see, the provost of Azusa Pacific University, with its thirty thousand students, admitted he had never known a time when APU wasn't there. Michael has added much to the university in his time there, but he didn't start it. And here is his presentation.

"David started Wesley Institute from nothing—no people, no college, not even the concept of a college. God called David to pioneer something that hadn't been done in Australia before.

"Education, in its broadest sense, incorporates any experience that has a formative effect on the mind, character, or ability of an individual. Educators facilitate such learning experiences, give intellectual, moral, and social instruction. This can be systematic instruction for a particular purpose, but we all know the empowering difference education makes when it engages the whole person in a mentoring, even discipling, relationship. This was Jesus's teaching style, and to this day, it is the process by which societies imprint their images and values on their young. This has also been David's teaching style—to stand or sit alongside and play/sing or write together—the teacher modeling and inspiring so the student is lifted into the company of the master, sharing in the joy of music making, feeling and experiencing the goals, and being empowered to reach for them. Not so much instruction as an infusion of skills, passion, and joy, a learning collaboration with skills caught rather than taught.

"International Educator of the Year. We would be here a very long time if we were to go through even a short list of graduates who not only learned their craft here but also caught something of David's pioneering spirit and dared to dream, trusting God to call, guide, and provide in new territories.

"Wesley Institute only exists because God gifted David, captivated his heart, gave him a kindred spirit in Marianna, and then gave him a vision so big it would take the rest of his life to fulfill.

"A missionary vision involved uprooting his family to a country and a lifestyle less affluent than his own.

"A pioneering vision, it involved going where no one around him had been and taking them with him.

"An educational vision involved the kind of sacrificial lifestyle that so many of you understand, focusing on teaching and empowering others.

"And a Christian vision, it gave rise to irrepressible joy and always some laughter, even in tough times.

"Perhaps the outcomes at the other end of the spectrum of this educational vision are even more wonderful. I'm thinking of those students who showed no promise and yet came to excel, those who came with talent and attitude and almost didn't make it anywhere but, at seemingly the last minute, woke up and became themselves and all those very ordinary students who continue to be inspired to greater things. We all know some of these and can rejoice at the miracles we see at Wesley Institute.

"David, we all celebrate this award that comes from the United States to one of its own citizens who left home with a call to enrich a neighbor in the southern hemisphere. You've paid a high price to change our world and to give each of us the chance to do what we enjoy. And you have taught us how ordinary people empowered by the spirit of God can indeed extend the known limits to transform lives and inspire to excellence.

"We salute you, and we praise God for you."

Words cannot express the gratitude I have for each staff member who encouraged and supported me throughout the years, and for those who shared my vision and worked tirelessly to help with whatever needed to be done. When I look back, I am amazed at the level of commitment and sacrifices that were made by so many, even just to work in such a place as Wesley Institute. But I have to especially thank Hilda Caine, who initially enrolled as a student in our first intake of students in 1983. She loved learning and soaked up almost all of the subjects we offered at the time. She gave her instructors and administration the impression she just couldn't get enough. She graduated and continued to grow academically, spiritually, intellectually, and in the knowledge of the Word.

I knew she had a busy schedule as a single mom, but she came back to see us and gifted us by volunteering where it was needed. There was something about the institute that drew our former students back to either volunteer or just say hi. That was the case with Hilda; she often volunteered to do what was needed.

I also remembered that she was a lover of books, so one day, I asked her if she would be interested in setting up a library. I thought she might at least think about it, but she immediately responded with a resounding, "Yes! I would love to!"

She demonstrated a consistent standard of excellence in everything she put her hand to. She became our first librarian. A few years later, she became the registrar of the institute and significantly contributed to building our reputation in the state and federal higher education departments as an institution that operated with genuine Christian ethics and with the highest integrity. She never lost her love for the library as it gave her the feeling of satisfaction in serving other students in their research projects and other academic work. At the same time, she kept her hand on the pulse of the library as it continued to expand and develop. It was also a feeling of satisfaction when she was able to acquire rare collections and resources in every field of study. Hilda's dedication and work will continue to enrich the lives of students for generations to come. God bless you, Hilda Caine!

International Educator of the Year—Awarded by Azusa Pacific University, presented by Provost, Dr. Michael Whyte, guest speaker at the 2009 Wesley Institute graduation ceremony in the Wesley Theatre

APPENDIX A

Administration
Reflections of My Time at Wesley Institute By Hilda Caine

After I had been seeking God for His direction for a couple of years, He led me to Wesley Institute. Then in its inaugural year (and known as IICM), I enrolled as a theology major with elective studies in music, the two fields closest to my heart. From the beginning, I was inspired, challenged, and encouraged to grow as a Christian in a dynamic, Spirit-filled academic community. Studying the Scriptures under Marianna Johnston and her team of wonderful lecturers and guest lecturers was truly amazing and has launched me on a lifelong love of the Word of God. And I have also grown in my deep appreciation of the creative and performing arts and seen how God uses these gifts to touch and change lives and even cultures. When I was a new member of Christian Life Centre, the *Easter Alive* production of 1984 was the first thing I saw, and I loved the joy of it—a way of telling the resurrection story that resonated with the theology and music in me.

That first year, IICM offered a higher education diploma in creative ministries with majors in music, dance, drama, visual arts, or theology; an integrative core; and provision for elective choices across majors. I still remember the buzz of studying theology under Marianna's management with a fine lineup of lecturers in this vibrant, creative environment and the joy of being able to also continue studying music electives. The typical year then included camps with international speakers (Winkie Pratney, Steve Fry, and Sy Rogers, to name a few), church placements, performances in the newly built entertainment center, and other smaller and larger artistic events—experiences that enriched my life.

I joined the college staff in 1984 and served in various positions until I retired in 2016. God affirmed my calling to this work many times during the years and blessed me beyond my expectations. I married David Caine, a fellow student, in 1988. Our two sons also studied at the college, Kevin as a music major and David as a theology major. Both Davids (my husband and son) became pastors, and Kevin works as a designer of interactive technology systems. The boys both found their wives in the Wesley Institute / Wesley Mission community. My response to the Holy Spirit's leading opened the gates to God's blessings for our children and now grandchildren.

I was privileged to serve with the college for thirty-two years, initially captivated by David's passion and joy in empowering his students and Marianna's insightful teaching of the Scriptures and then inspired by the many wonderful lecturers who transformed students' lives and enabled them to follow their callings and change their worlds. We all walked in richness because God gave David a vision and he came here to include us in it.

My journey with David and Marianna Johnston commenced in February 1984, the college's inaugural year. I enrolled as a theology major with elective studies in music. By the end of that year, I had also joined the staff—a decision that changed my life.

A member of the Christian Life Centre congregation, I had witnessed something of the heartbeat that had brought David and Marianna to Australia to pioneer an accredited college of higher education in theology and creative arts with studies structured to facilitate integration between disciplines. This was unique at a time when a candidate for parish ministry could only be accredited by completing the theological course of a particular denomination. Any form of integration, or even dialogue between denominations, was regarded with suspicion.

However, David's call was from the Lord; and the vision grew and gained momentum with many gifted people joining the staff, designing and developing curriculum, teaching, mentoring, and managing the various aspects of the growing educational community. By 1998, the college was offering bachelor's degrees, accredited by the government, in music, dance, drama, visual arts, and graphic design and postgraduate diplomas in counseling and education. Degrees in theology were accredited with the Sydney College of Divinity. Over the next few years, accredited master's degrees in theology, music, counseling, and education expanded the college offerings.

Then I think about the staff through the years—amazing people drawn to an amazing vision. So many out there are pioneer educators, creating and forging new ground in ways their university peers don't get the opportunity to do. How many people actually get to write degrees from scratch, from just a seed of an idea, and research, publish, perform, create, teach, model, support, and transform students' lives? This is a wonder and a privilege. And we walk in this richness together because one man had a vision from God and came here to include us in it. In following the Lord's leading, David pioneered something so wonderful and passed the baton to others so that it still lives. Quite honestly, I don't know of anything to parallel it in Christian higher education.

With passion, joy, great wisdom, and courage, David and Marianna Johnston created a very special learning community in which we all experienced the pleasure of God in fields of endeavor that embraced the academic and the artistic, creative, and innovative. We were each stretched, enriched, and changed. And as we worshiped, learned, and grew together, we all came to see how

> Christ plays in ten thousand places,
> Lovely in limbs, and lovely in eyes not his
> To the Father through the features of men's faces.
> (Gerard Manly Hopkins, *As Kingfishers Catch Fire, Dragonflies Draw Flame,* 1877)

APPENDIX B

Australia Studies Centre

Dear Dr. J,

I wanted to send you a note of gratitude as I feel as though I must tell you how truly I have enjoyed my time in Australia and particularly at Wesley. God has revealed a lot to me this semester, and Wesley has played a major part in that. Wesley has shown me it's not about the size of the facilities or a place but the heart of the people that make up the institution. I have met a lot of interesting people at Wesley, many with passionate hearts for God to change the world. Secondly, I encountered at Wesley, claiming the arts for Christ, as I feel I have really caught that vision in my time at Wesley.

So I guess I am writing to thank you, Dr. J, for your vision, investment, and passion for Wesley and the ASC Program. I know there are many others that feel similarly as well. So thank you from all of us who have grown, been stretched, and nurtured by our experiences at Wesley as God has certainly blessed it.

With gratitude,
Caitlin Connolly
USA

APPENDIX C

Faculty

I just wanted to say that I meant what I said, that you were and continue to be my mentor. All you taught me and all you modeled as our leader still guide me in what I do.

What has really hit me of late is your confidence in me to lead and disciple my young students. I remember you saying to me to be like the mother hen who gathers her chicks in her wings. I will never forget that.

So for the last four years, I have been leading women's ministries at church, and all the pastoring/discipling you allowed me to do for the dancers has really enabled me to lead this ministry. Same sort of issues—confidence, having a voice, working through serious life issues (abuse, disorders, relationships, and direction in life), and being an advocate for them. Many are creative but have needed an avenue to pursue this with confidence. Such a blessing to me to be by their side as they unleash their creativity for God.

You have enabled God's work in me and in all of us. And of course, this goes for Marianna too. The two of you side by side and with Marianna teaching us the Bible and more—formidable.

—Evelyn Defina, head, School of Dance, 1998–2007

He was such an inspirational man as head of Wesley Institute for the Arts and many times introduced choreographies performed under the Christian dance umbrella at Wesley Theatre (opposite the Hilton in town). A few of my choreographies were performed there. David talked to me through text to say that he enjoyed my concepts and dance works!

—Mira Mansell, dance choreographer at large

APPENDIX D

Comments From Former Students at Wesley Institute for Ministry and the Arts

Graduates were inspired to walk tall in the footsteps of giants in their fields and asked how Wesley Institute has influenced them.

Victoria Govers, GradDipEd (Secondary), BM, Master of Teaching (Teaches primary specializing in literacy and English as a second language in K-6 and private studio vocal teacher)

I was absolutely terrified turning up for my audition at Wesley Institute in 2005. I was in the midst of my HSC in Wollongong, and it felt like my whole future was riding on the two songs I was about to present. David Johnston and Heva Chan sat across from me, looking at their paperwork and awaiting my presentation. My backing track began, and I opened my mouth to sing "Wishing You Were Somehow Here Again" from *Phantom*. As I began to sing, DJ's head snapped up, eyes wide, and jaw dropped.

Oh no! Is that a good reaction? Have I completely messed this up already? Am I the worst singer he has heard so far?

He was so attentive throughout my song. I couldn't figure out if it was a good thing or not. When I finished, he looked at Heva, and I heard him say the name Christa. Who was that? I proceeded to sing another piece, this time an Edith Piaf medley. When I was done, DJ asked me if I had any questions.

"When will I know if I have been successful or not?"

Wide-eyed again, he smiled and said, "Oh! You're in! You're definitely in!"

I couldn't believe it.

"Oh! I just need you to complete the aural part of the audition!" He strolled over to the piano and played a few intervals.

"Um, minor second?" I said with not a hint of confidence.

He looked at me in a way I would soon grow to be familiar with. "It's okay," he said. "We can work on that!"

I came from a troubled family. I had two alcoholic parents. My mother was in and out of my life; my father was extremely critical, destructive, and controlling. I had spent my last two years in a youth refuge, women's refuge, and crisis accommodation. I was in desperate need of stability and guidance when I left school. Wesley Institute was the perfect place for me. My friends became my family, and my lecturers became my mentors. DJ was the father of the college and the heart and the soul, and every choir rehearsal felt like a family gathering. For me, it was three years of home—a home I had always longed for. We even did international holidays together and won awards at the same time! I know, along with myself, that every student who had the privilege of learning with DJ looks back on their time at Wesley as fondly as I do and wishes they could relive those years all over again.

Noel Johnston, Music

Noel Johnston, David and Marianna's son and one of the early graduates of Wesley Institute, completed a bachelor of music in studio guitar in the United States at USC, completed a master's degree in jazz guitar at the University of North Texas, released his own album recorded at the Sydney Opera House recording studio, performed on over forty others, wrote a musical, performs live on Daystar TV, teaches at the University of North Texas, is in high demand as a session player, published three editions of *Voicing Modes* and *Modal*

Etudes for jazz guitar, and—with his wife, Jiyoung—runs their own music school, the Lone Star Music Academy in Flower Mound, Texas.

Merrill Wong, GradDip in Counseling

Wesley Institute has given me a whole new lease on life and a brand-new career at a mature age, and it wasn't until I left to do more study somewhere else that I realized just how excellent the teaching was at WI.

Rachel Outhred, Music

Having completed the bachelor of music at Wesley Institute, she went on to complete a master's in international development in London and then a PhD in international law. She was sponsored to travel to West Africa to research a form of modern-day slavery that affects women and is seeking to develop a model by which African communities can be empowered to find ways to eliminate the cultural norms that legitimate violence against women. She teaches first-year undergrads in the Centre for Teaching Excellence in Human Rights, Social Justice, and Citizenship at Roehampton University, working with NGOs to develop the curricula for a BA in human rights and MA in human rights practice.

Lisa Wilson, Dance

Lisa Wilson added to her dance degree a master of education in dance and then conducted dance residencies at the University of Wyoming. Currently serving as assistant director of the School of Dance at the Edna Manley College of the Visual and Performing Arts in Kingston, Jamaica, Lisa teaches dance and plays an active role in curriculum planning and development. With her husband, Kurt, also a dancer, Lisa established Art Streams, a ministry that provides dance training (modern contemporary and jazz for intermediate and advanced levels) in weekly technique classes, summer camps, and professional productions. Their vision is to serve as a model of how faith and art can be professionally integrated.

Asked about the greatest lessons she had learned, Lisa said, "Success involves a sound trust in the Author of our lives, risk taking, discipline, and self-belief. I can assuredly state that the spiritual and artistic foundations established in my life through my studies at Wesley Institute and the steps I have taken to build on those foundations have shaped my confidence as a Christian artist in the marketplace today."

Linden Jones, Music

The main thing for me is that I have grown a lot as a person, built up my self-esteem, and helped myself discover things I never knew about myself. I think that is one of the best things that has happened. My education at Wesley Institute has changed my life, and meeting and studying under esteemed musicians and having great lecturers have been a blessing.

Tamara Smith, Dance

It has brought me to a realization that dance is an excelling experience, and the teachers and staff have brought me to a very high standard of dance that I have been happy with. And it has brought me to a point where I can go out into the secular world and really excel in the techniques that I have developed at Wesley.

Coming to Wesley has changed my life with God, showing me that He can be in all aspects of your life and, in everything you do, He is always there helping you and showing you; and that is what Wesley has shown me throughout my time at Wesley.

Nerida Lane, GradDip in Counseling

I have enjoyed my years at Wesley immensely, and I am going to miss them. I've had such fellowship, friendship, learning, and growth and hope it will all continue in the future; but it's hard to find that many mature people. I wouldn't say I'm an eclectic counselor having learned all those theories. I would say I am a Christian counselor, and having an understanding of how God sees us, I can then use the others as skills.

Missy Johnston, Graphic Design

I am David and Marianna's daughter, and I completed a BTh and diploma in graphic design at Wesley Institute. I went on to become a secondary school teacher in the United States teaching Bible and graphics.

Tim Matta, Graphic Design

Now graduating from design, when I first came to Wesley Institute, I honestly did not like the place spiritually because I was far from being a Christian. It has taken me somewhere I haven't really been before and has shown me what Christianity and Jesus is all about, and for that, I am really grateful. At first, it was very abstract, and I didn't understand. But it has changed me, and I am now a calmer and gentler person. And I am a more forgiving and understanding person thanks to Wesley Institute. I am currently designing in a design studio at Surry Hills. I am enjoying it, and it is a great experience and fun. I am designing for some big international clients—for example, Breville—and am getting great exposure.

Chris Stewart, Music

As a music graduate, Wesley Institute has given me vision and skill and has prepared me for the things to come. I am planning to pursue music professionally. I am a songwriter, singer, and guitarist and would like to continue my songwriting, produce albums, and hopefully impact and tour Australia-wide. Tonight I am doing a CD launch of my first album.

Matthew Bourne, Music

I graduated with a bachelor of arts in performance, majoring in music ministry. Wesley Institute has given me a home that I never thought I would have. It has shown me what I am capable of as a person and in Christ and has trained my skills in ways that I had no idea that it would. Wesley Institute has affected my spiritual life. It has taught me amazing things about God and challenged my preconceptions about the world and how God relates to our world. I am committed to continuing my pursuit of finding work in the music industry and continue playing.

Heidi Bornerman, Dance

The most affecting thing in my life at Wesley Institute has been the people and the relationships we built. It wasn't just an education in terms of technical learning but in life development that was most important to me. We learned a lot technically in our dance and a lot academically in our study of the Old and New Testaments. We grew spiritually and also in the way we relate to each other, and the strength of having brotherly and sisterly love around you is so important.

Naomi Buchanan, Drama

Wesley Institute has changed me greatly. It has been three years of maturing and spiritual growth not only in my Christian development but in myself. I believe I am now the woman God wants me to be. I have a lot more growing to do, but I definitely grew toward God, which is awesome. It is definitely the biggest thing that Wesley has done for me personally. Skills-wise and acting-wise, there is a huge difference, and I think this is because of the encouragement I got through the faculty. Acting is very hard, and the encouragement and knowing the support is there have been a huge help. I am teaching drama full-time at the moment and hope to continue that but am also looking at doing a DipEd in special needs.

CONCEIVING THE INCONCEIVABLE

Julian Pearson, Drama

I have turned into a man of God foremost, and I have been able to learn things that I wouldn't have had the opportunity to if I hadn't been at Wesley Institute. My education has meant more to me than I can really express in words. It's been great. It has prepared me for a career immensely. There have been things that we have learned in our studies that I have spoken to people with degrees from other universities about. They have not yet learned these, so we are a real step ahead.

Tim Wells, Drama

Wesley Institute was a major part of my life, and I think I have grown from being a fairly nice kid into a man, hopefully. It has been a major, central part of who I am as a person. I have learned so much and have grown spiritually. It has helped my skills and has been a turning point in my life as well as for other people here at Wesley. It has meant a great deal to me, and I will always hold it dear to my heart. I have found work with the Parramatta Riverside Theatre and work in other theaters as well, and it has been a jumping board for me into theater.

Alison Rubie, Drama

Before I came to Wesley, I was nervous about what I was supposed to do in life and where God was leading me; and since then, it has enriched my life not only in my education but with friends and extended family. Getting to know God more and more and more, I am looking forward to where He is leading me in the future. I intend to travel to England at the end of the year to pursue my career in the performing arts and theater.

Megan Simpson, Drama

Coming to Wesley Institute has had a big impact on my life. Originally I wanted to go to drama school; but coming to a Christian college has impacted me because, for the first time in my life in presenting my graduation piece, I actually relied on God totally for the outcome. I really felt His peace, the power of His patience with me, His love, and the fact that He is there when you most need Him. I've grown spiritually. I've had a rocky time, but I've enjoyed it immensely.

Dwayne Hickman, Theology

The great thing about Wesley Institute was that learning about theology and the environment kept you grounded in the real world. It's something different about learning with musicians and dancers and keeping theology in places where it matters instead of in ivory towers. That was the best part of Wesley for me. I am now a lawyer with a firm in the city. I did a law/theology degree, and I think I'll practice law for a while, then do something else with theology.

Hailey Joy Barrett, Drama

I was the valedictorian and a drama graduate. My spiritual growth at Wesley has been amazing, and this came from the community that Wesley was and is. Learning to serve one another, love one another, and listen to and overcome difficulties helped me and encouraged me. I was really nurtured at Wesley; academically I was pushed and encouraged to strive to do my best always. It has been a terrific experience. The teachers are really committed to helping you in both a professional and friendly way. They are very professional and skillful in their chosen fields.

Amanda Langford, Graphic Design

Wesley Institute has changed my life. I came to Wesley a bit unsure about my faith in God and not knowing what I wanted to do as a career, and the guidance and support there have been really amazing. Everyone there has this love for each other and care for each other, and the staff is really amazing. I really loved every minute that I was there, and I'm really sad that I'm graduating. It has put me ahead in leaps and bounds by having lecturers who really know their stuff and who really cared for me as well. My major was graphic design, and I want to get into a firm in Darwin and also get into teaching graphic design and art and working with youth and using the skills that I have learned at Wesley.

Nicola Simpson, Masters in Counseling

Being at Wesley Institute has changed my life, and I'll never be the same. I have met people here who have guided me, installed a vision, and also given me a way of thinking where nothing is impossible. God has really blessed me through the people and the friends I have made here, and the staff has been incredible. They have been there in times of difficulty and in times of amazing joy, and it has just been a family away from home. I am from Scotland, but now I really think I would really like to work with people who had been involved with abuse in some way and would like to be able to minister to them in a practical way but also bring Jesus to them in a way that can change their lives. I hope that that can be a way that God can change me in the future. I really don't know where He is going to take me, but that is my vision. I'm sure He knows where my heart is and if I'm suitable for that area.

Laura Smith, Graphic Design

For me who was a graphic design major, Wesley means to me that I have been able to expand one of my passions, photography, as well as graphic design. I now leave with both of those backing me up, and I hope to get a job using both of these working for a magazine.

Wilma Eileen, GradDip in Counseling, Theology

Armed with the GradDip in counseling a few years back, Wilma returned to Fiji and runs the West Fiji branch of the Fiji Women's Crisis Centre. She and her six staff members offer free nonjudgmental counseling to women and children. The center was nominated in 2007 for a United Nations Human Rights Award for its "bravery and courage in the face of threats and intimidation, for protecting and defending the rights of Fiji citizens, specifically the rights of women and children, from violence and oppression, as well as being a leading advocacy organization for democracy and justice for all."

She enjoyed the BTh at Wesley because it involved the creative arts, and she was able to explore things that she didn't know existed. She hopes to be able to carry these to Fiji, where she can use her ministry/counseling with high school students and involve them creatively in drama and music because this is what she discovered at Wesley that had been hidden in her for a long time.

Dean Terry, Drama

I graduated with an advanced diploma in drama. I wish there were more students who could go to Wesley because I learned so much, I grew so much, and I developed as a person so much. I could not have done this without the help of staff, my Lord God, family, and friends. The way that I was pushed to go to the edge and keep going and got up in front of an audience and spoke and took part in the play *Back from Nowhere* at the Opera House was an amazing step for me, to get up in front of so many people and do a play that would help others. My dream or my passion is to put what I have learned at Wesley into practice to help me with my clowning and my mime and to develop in the creative arts. I want to help people in the community and the church to develop the creative arts through clowning and mime. I will be on tour soon traveling through Queensland performing at large Christian events and wherever I can be used by God. That is my dream: to be used by God wherever I go.

Glenys Wheatley, Music, 1988

> *The effectual fervent prayer of a righteous man availeth much.*
> —James 5:16

Few people have influence in our lives as teachers do. If, however, we have the privilege to sit under the tutelage of a godly teacher, we are most blessed of all students.

Such was Dr. David Johnston—concert violinist, visionary, director of the college the International Institute for Creative Ministries (IICM), but, more than this, a humble servant of the Lord—always preferring to just be called David.

My acceptance letter to IICM was personally written by David. It took this form:

> Normally we would advise that you continue your violin studies for one more year before we accept you to study at IICM. However, having prayed about this, I personally feel in the Holy Spirit that we should accept you this year to the college.

Therefore, it was in January 1987 that I packed up my life in New Zealand and moved to Australia to study violin under the wonderful guiding hand of David Johnston.

I must say those years as a student were most challenging but, at the same time, most gratifying, laying the foundation for years of ministry to come. The institute was, like many Bible colleges, a melting pot of talents. But so much more than that. We, as creative artists, were given the ability to dream in ways that had previously not been embraced by many of the churches we had come from. First and foremost, we were all followers of Christ and secondly musicians, visual artists, dancers, poets, Bible students, and more. The core value of the institute was excellence—the excellence of character, excellence in our walk with Christ, and the building block for excellence in the outworking of our individual gifts. The values of David as the director became the values of the college and, in turn, our inheritance as students.

Now in 2021, I can look back at that time as the foundation of all of the ministries that followed. Having only begun studying violin at age twenty-five, God's gift to me was a godly teacher with vision who not only taught me the excellence of violin but also the excellence of character and the value of the one life we have in Christ that we can pour out for Him.

And so since graduating from IICM, I have played in orchestras all over the whole world and ministered in churches in Australia, Israel (both Israeli and Arab), Morocco, Spain, England, America, Serbia, Azerbaijan, and Turkey. And lastly but not finally, I have been passing on my inheritance to other Christ-following musicians. Some are now serving the Lord with their gifts in many different parts of the world, and some are still in the process.

All of this is because of the vision of one man: Dr. David Johnston, teacher and friend.

Dr. Anthony Clarke, Master of Music

My time at Wesley Institute and how the lessons learned helped shape my life and career. I can understand any institution rejoicing in the success of former students, especially if that success has not been insignificant. To adequately respond would take considerably more words than I'm allowed, and more importantly, I feel that my response should not concern me but rather focus on the people who helped shape my life. With specific reference to myself, all I will say is that my time at WI helped me forge a career in music that has led me to be fortunate to conduct, perform, teach, and be associated with a number of leading institutions in various countries. I hope that I have enriched the lives of those people I have worked with and the audiences who have listened.

So did my time at WI benefit me? Yes, but now we must deal with the crux of the matter. What is WI, or for that matter, what is any institution? Is it the bricks and mortar, the physical structure? Maybe. Is it the teaching staff? To an extent, yes. Is it the students? Once again, to an extent, yes. Is it the community contained within the institution? Now we're getting closer. For me, WI always has been and always will be David and Marianna Johnston. Without David and Marianna, WI would never have existed and would never have succeeded in touching the lives of so many people. From the seed that initiated the idea to the institution's inception and its fruition, David and Marianna have been its heart and soul. WI is David and Marianna Johnston.

The only reason I attended WI was to learn from David. His wealth of musical knowledge came from an impressive pedagogical line. As he has been influenced by preeminent teachers such as Ivan Galamian, Jascha Heifetz, Yehudi Menuhin, and Alice Schoenfeld, David's credentials are impeccable. Key components of David's teaching style revolved around his great love of music and people. His teaching imbued warmth and compassion, coupled with high expectations and strong self-discipline. He was strict regarding adherence to the printed text and constantly reminded me of the diligence required to achieve high-level performances within the public domain.

The most powerful lessons I learned during my time at WI revolved around not only music but also life. Both David and Marianna always led by example; that was their secret. Their love and genuine care for individuals, their love of imparting knowledge, their joy for life, and their love of the Word—all these values they cherished and devoted themselves to; and all those who were fortunate enough to meet them couldn't help but be touched by their love and sincerity. When it was time for my future wife, Bili, and I to marry, it was David and Marianna we asked to conduct the ceremony. This was such a memorable experience, one we both continue to cherish. When Bili and I have been fortunate, we always want to share the news with David and Marianna; and when life takes an unexpected turn, once again, it is our dear friends we turn to.

How does one measure success? Is it the amount of money a person makes? Is it the number of graduates who go on to have significant careers? No, it's the number of people whose lives have been touched and who, in turn, will go on to help change the lives of others. I believe one of the main reasons for the success of WI was that David and Marianna viewed it as an extension of their family.

So thank you, both. Thank you for taking the time to dream and for turning your dream into reality. Thank you for taking the time to care and for giving us a place where we could learn within a caring environment, a place that was able to help so many people. Thank you for your love and friendship.

With love and gratitude,
Dr. Anthony Clarke, BA, MMusic, PhD

*****

I never could have achieved bringing the conception of an institution like Wesley Institute into existence without the support of the many loyal faculty, staff, administration, and especially my wife, Marianna, and family both in Australia and in the United States. Without the strings attached to God and those who believed in me and my vision, none of this would have been possible. All of it has been and continues to be for the cause of Christ through the lives and ministry of its graduates, who are spread to the four corners of the world in over forty nations.

ABOUT THE AUTHOR

Dr. David Johnston, Violinist

Who could imagine a college where you could major in integrating the arts with theology?

Close friends and colleagues said to David, "You won't be able to start a college like that! It's not something you've done before or know how to do. Americans are not that well received in Australia. You will surely fail."

Indeed, he had no choice but to go in blind faith and the strength of God to "conceive the *inconceivable*."

In his memoirs, it will become apparent why even his closest friends thought that what he was attempting to do was impossible and couldn't conceive why he would move his whole family to Australia. You will follow some of the unbelievable yet exciting and miraculous stories that spanned a period of almost thirty years. He was expecting to be there for only two, but what kept him and his family there for many years is brought to light.

It brought to light the passages in Scripture that "nothing is impossible with God" and the following:

> But God hath chosen the foolish things of the world to confound the wise, and God hath chosen the weak things of the world to confound the things which are mighty. (1 Corinthians 1:27 KJV)

What started in his early days in Sydney moved from a feeling of being ridiculed for seeking government recognition for accreditation of his courses to subsequently, at the end of his time there, representing the government himself by serving on accreditation panels for tertiary and state university courses and a PhD panel at the University of Sydney. This was a great sense of achievement and fulfillment.

David has authored several articles published in music journals. Based on his innovative approach to higher education, his paper published under the title *The Sustainability of Private Christian Higher Education* was presented by him to international educators at the Global Educators' Forum in Tainan City Women's College of Technology and Arts in Tainan City, Taiwan, in April 2004.

David and Marianna have been married for more than fifty years and have three married children and seven grandchildren. They met in church and taught in the same school district. David taught instrumental music in grades 4–12 in the Sacramento City School District, where Marianna also taught.

After marrying and moving to Bakersfield, David became an associate professor of music at Bakersfield College, head of the string department, lecturer in musicology, and conductor of the college community orchestra and later concurrently served as music director in their church, the next stepping-stone in his calling. He now teaches violin at his son's music academy in Dallas, Texas.

It is usual for David to speak with individuals about his life Down Under with exuberance and passion. His relational style and personal experiences bring warmth to his writing and reveal his love for sharing his vision.

Only one life, 'twill soon be past. Only what's done for Christ will last.

www.ingramcontent.com/pod-product-compliance
Lightning Source LLC
Chambersburg PA
CBHW042128160426
43198CB00021B/2946